LONG SHOTS FROM THE FLATLANDS

LONG SHOTS FROM THE FLATLANDS

by
Richard Wiman

with artwork by
Lisa Brunetti

**Published by
Greasy Bayou Publishing Co.
P.O. Box 73
Belzoni, MS 39038**

Printed in the United States of America by

Jostens Publishing Company
401 Science Park Road
State College, PA 16801

ISBN #

Designed and produced by Julian Toney

CIP data pending

DEDICATION

This book is dedicated to the people of Belzoni and surrounding areas and the members of The First Presbyterian Church of Belzoni, Mississippi. Good churches can be found all over the world, but the Lord could not have called me to a greater group of people than the people of The First Presbyterian Church in the Heart of the Delta and Catfish Capital of the World. Though I would like to mention names, I'm afraid I'd leave someone really special out if I did, so I'll just mention four very special women. Without their love and support, I don't know where I'd be, but I doubt I'd be in your den right now in the form of this book! Therefore, in the most special way I know how, I dedicate this work to my wife and best friend, Dorothy, and to my three wonderful daughters, Ruth, Joy, and Lindsay. Now if you call our house and hear, "Hello, A Little Bit of Heaven, which little angel do you wish to speak to?" you'll fully understand. In addition, I also want to dedicate this work to the memory of two special men of God, Rev. Mike Sartelle and his young son, Nate, who were killed in an automobile accident on January 1, 1992. May God bless and keep his family.

TABLE OF CONTENTS

7

INTRODUCTION

Total surprise — was the most often expressed reaction when this author's first book appeared in print. Pastoring a small-town church in the Mississippi Delta doesn't do much for name recognition. People who know me couldn't believe I could write funny stories, and the rest of the world didn't know me at all.

After the surprise factor faded, people began expressing their delight and joy with the work entitled, <u>Tired Tubes and Ten-Speed Turkeys</u>. They were thoroughly entertained and pleased with their investments of time and money. One set of pleased parents told me that mine was the first book their son had ever read in its entirety. Allowing as how he was nineteen years old, that was quite a compliment.

Members of the Southeastern Outdoor Press Association recognized my first contribution to our Southern heritage of outdoor humor by awarding the book Third Place in the Excellence in Craft competition for Outdoor Book of the Year for 1992. Needless to say, the honor was a thrill, a total surprise, and a great encouragement to this fledgling fiddler with words.

A newspaper column was born out of all the hoopla over that first book and the award. "Long Shots" first appeared in the "Belzoni Banner" in January of 1992 and occasionally in other Delta papers such as the "Tunica Times" and the "Deer Creek Pilot."

Reactions to the column have been mighty encouraging, which is why you're now reading this introduction to <u>Long Shots from the Flatlands</u>. Where did the title for the column and book

9

come from? Well sir . . .

Would you say the odds of a three-legged horse getting into the Kentucky Derby might be considered a long shot? Harry Truman was considered, by political analysts of his day, as a long shot to win the Presidency, but we all know what happened to "The Buck Stops Here" Harry, don't we?

Long shots are everywhere. Making a million bucks off this book is a long shot. Taking a world class whitetail buck at 400 yards or landing a ten-pound largemouth on six-pound test line are both considered long shots.

What's the point? Sometimes, the long shots in life, no matter how impossible the odds seem, come through. Somebody always wins the lottery and somebody always takes home the prize. We're all familiar with long shots. This work takes a look at a whole banana clip full of long shots from the perspective of the Mississippi Delta. For those of you not familiar with this part of the country, the mighty Mississippi River fanned out hundreds of thousands of times before the Army Corps of Engineers built levees to make it behave. The annual floods built a rich alluvial plain, nearly as flat as a flitter (whatever a flitter is). These stories of long shots from this flatland range from the long shot of taking a wild turkey with a boat paddle to landing a bobwhite quail and an eight-pound largemouth bass at the same time.

At some points along the way, you're going to say, "This guy's pullin' my leg." You know what? I will be, but you may never know for sure when it's happening. You see, figuring out whether you're reading fact or fiction may prove to be a long shot for you.

One thing's for sure, you're going to hear a certain statement made over and over again in this book. Don't quit reading it just because you've read it before. Keep reading it, because the message it conveys is an important one for your life and mine.

What is this statement? Well, if you turn on over to the first chapter in just a minute and get started, you'll find out soon enough.

Along the way, you're going to laugh, shake your head, and sometimes shed a tear. At times you'll sit back and reflect on your own experiences and responsibilities. Whatever else you do with this book, read it and share it with a friend. Don't let this book gather dust. Shucks, this thing might even end up changing your whole life.

"A long shot," you say? Well, whatever you do, don't be afraid to go with the long shots. Live life to its fullest every moment and be ready! Be ready, for the Good Lord is going to call us all one of these days, and that, my friend, is no long shot.

LONG SHOTS FROM THE FLATLANDS

by Richard Wiman
pastor, Boy Scout leader,
outdoorsman, school
chaplain, counselor
and friend

13

"Now a certain man drew a bow at random, and struck the King of Israel between the joints of his armor." (I Kings 22:34a)

A LONG SHOT

The hunt started out just like hundreds before. There was a long, narrow wheat field, early morning fog, frosty air, and a slight breeze out of the northwest. Perfect. This was going to be a memorable morning. I could feel it in my bones, or was that the frosty air I was feeling?

Sitting rather comfortably with my back against a small cottonwood tree (at Fitler, a cottonwood tree farm owned by James River Corporation), a doe seemed to appear, like the Phantom of the Opera, out of thin air (thick would describe the fog better).

The heifer just seemed to materialize right there in the middle of the wheat field, though I knew she couldn't have done so. Suddenly, another deer was following right behind her—a spike buck. I watched intently as they ghosted across the field in a matter of seconds, never running, steadily walking. Then they were gone, and my pulse started to return to normal.

A long half-hour passed. Sleep invaded my world and threatened my vigil. I roused from my dreams several times, once to see another doe just as she reached the trees on the opposite edge of the field from me. The cross-hairs of my rifle met her shoulder as I touched the trigger ever so lightly. The rifle boomed, the deer barreled out of the field, seemingly unhurt. "I couldn't have missed!"

After fruitlessly searching for evidence of a hit and thus ruining the spot, or so I reckoned, I returned to my comfortable seat. In less than fifteen minutes, I had watched a nice six-point buck pass within thirty steps of my tree and missed another doe with the same less-than-perfect marksmanship. "The scope must be off," I concluded. "It couldn't be my aim!"

Disgusted with my performance or the rifle's, whichever, I decided a long, slow walk through the cottonwoods might prove successful. The sun was well up by now and so was the temperature.

When I finally returned to the truck after an hour or so, I began to change out of my heavy clothes. Off came the wool sweater, wool shirt, wool pants, longjohns, and wool boot socks (told you it was frosty).

As I sat down on the truck seat to catch my breath and put on some light-weight cotton socks, I noticed a deer had entered the field. The animal was so far down at the other end of the field that I couldn't tell with my naked eye (just about everything was naked at that moment) whether it was a doe or a buck. Putting on my hunting hat (don't ask why I did that), I eased out of the pickup and took my rifle off the hood.

Turning the scope up to 8-power, I checked her out. Yes, she was a nice, fat doe, just what I was looking for that morning. Since James River had told us to kill some 325 does, I had to do my part, don't you see?

I dropped my pants on the ground so I could have a comfortable, dry seat — before and after the shot. Anyhow, the sitting position is much steadier with your pants down!

Knowing that she was a long way off, I placed the cross-hairs on top of her head and squeezed. With the recoil of my rifle, the deer disappeared from the scope. "Did I miss — again?" I wondered out loud with a tinge of disgust.

Dressing quickly, I stepped off the distance to the soon-to-be table fare. The shot had been 375 steps, strides like those of Bill Allen, whom everybody in Belzoni concedes as having the longest, most distinctive strides of anyone around.

Don't ask me how I did it. How did I hit something at that distance when I had missed twice at less than half that yardage? Do you suppose that I may have been over dressed on the first two shots?

Seriously, I don't know if there is a moral or lesson to this story ("Go with the bare necessities" would be the lesson if there were one), or any relevant information about how to dress for a successful deer hunt. Taking a deer with your pants down may be a long shot for me and for you, but...

Whatever you do, don't be afraid to go with the long shots. Live life to its fullest every moment and be ready!

In the spring of the year . . .

"Now a watchman stood on the tower of Jezreel, and he saw the company of Jehu as he came, and said, 'I see a company of men.' And Joram said, 'Get a horseman and send him to meet them, and let him say, "Is it peace?"' 'So the horseman went to meet him, and said, 'Thus says the king: "Is it peace?"' 'And Jehu said, 'What have you to do with peace? Turn around and follow me.' And the watchman reported, saying, 'The messenger went to them, but is not coming back.' Then he sent out a second horseman who came to them, and said, 'Thus says the king, "Is it peace?"' 'And Jehu answered, 'What have you to do with peace? Turn around and follow me.' And the watchman reported, saying, 'He went up to them and is not coming back; and the driving is like the driving of Jehu the son of Nimshi, for he drives furiously!'" (II Kings 9:17-20)

LEARNING TO DRIVE

Almost from the time of birth, we seem to have the innate desire to learn to drive. Just take a look at the toys you've bought for your children or grandchildren lately.

The first toys we bought our girls included a combination, bell-ringing, noise-making, radio-tuning knob, and a tiny steering wheel. We all put our little tykes in strollers, walkers, and wagons before they can stand on their own two feet.

One of the proudest moments daddies have in life is the day little Johnny or Jennifer, whichever the case may be, rides down the road in the truck with us. We're so proud that they can now ride with Daddy.

Not long after their first excursions with us in the truck, they start asking if they can sit in our lap and steer. In the blink of an eye, they've grown enough to sit behind the wheel and reach the pedals, and from that point on it's, "LOOK OUT WORLD!"

Our oldest turned fourteen the summer of 1991, which meant the urge to drive became overwhelming. Everytime we started to go somewhere that summer, we heard, "Can I drive?"

I remember when I first started to learn how to drive. My friends living out in the country had been driving since they were mere children, but us town urchins had to wait until we were thirteen or fourteen before we got our chance.

Back in the dark ages of the late fifties and early sixties, most cars had standard transmissions. Learning to drive with a standard transmission was really a trip.

Daddy was the first to take a turn at teaching me how to drive. I still remember him taking me to the parking lot behind the high school, telling me all about the gear shift positions, the proper way to use the clutch, gas and brake pedals. At that age, I wasn't listening to anything he said. Constantly interrupting his instructions with, "I already know that, Dad," I was totally unprepared for the first attempt. As it turned out, so was Daddy.

That first effort was like sitting in the cockpit of an airplane during the pre-flight check list.

"Gear shift in neutral?"

"Check."

"Clutch in?"

"Check."

"Gas pedal slightly depressed?"

"Check."

"Mirror adjusted?"

"Check."

"Seatbelt fastened?"

"Check."

"Left hand on wheel, right hand on key?"

"Check!"

"Okay, I guess we're ready. Start her up, son."

"Hey Dad, how come you got that crash helmet on?"

"Don't worry about it. Just start the car."

Ignition went smoothly. I had my foot on the gas pedal a little too much, but Dad said it was good for the car every now and then to have the soot blown out of the carburetor.

With clutch depressed, I pulled the shift lever on the column toward the wheel and down into the position for first gear. That accomplished, I eased off the clutch, or at least I thought I eased off.

The car bucked like a rodeo bull. After several lurches and

jerks, the car kind of whimpered and died.

"Rough, huh Dad? Dad?" Where'd he go anyway? That first sudden and unexpected jerk sent him to the floorboard of the back seat for cover. After a few seconds of calm, assured that we had come safely to a stop, he peeked over the seat.

"Son, maybe we need some more instruction on the coordination between clutch and gas pedals."

The next day, we tried again. Everything went much more smoothly. With the car running quietly, we eased off in first gear without a hitch.

The transition from first to second gear wasn't so slick. Instead of shifting from first to second, I went from first to reverse, or at least tried to. The gear shift hit reverse with the worst grinding sound, and the car shuddered all over. I quickly glanced at Dad, and he was empathizing with the car. He was shuddering as well — peering over the seat from the back again.

Leaving out some of the more choice expressions (which he didn't leave out), he said, "Son, get out of the car." We changed places, and he drove home. That was the last driving lesson I had from my Dad.

After that, driving lessons fell to my mother. From lessons sitting in the living room floor with three books, each representing one of the pedals, I learned to let out on the clutch and ease in on the gas at the same time, thus insuring a smooth start. I learned that second gear is half-way up, out, and then up again, thus opening the way for a driving career that I longed for more than anything I could imagine at the tender age of fourteen.

The time came for me to teach my oldest. She mastered the car with its automatic transmission with no sweat. Speed was and is a bit of a problem (like her mother in that regard), like it is for all of us during our teenage years. Some of us never get over the love for speed!

The standard transmission in the truck is another story. We've tried a time or two to learn how to handle the gears, but after a few lurches with no back seat to hide in, I've decided we'll just wait a while on the standard transmission. I think I'll let Mother teach Ruth, Joy, and Lindsay! On second thought, I love my truck too much for that. Maybe I'll just tell them to stick with automatic transmissions.

Learning to drive may not be a long shot for you teenagers. But teaching you how to handle a standard transmission can be a real long shot for us parents, but...

Whatever you do, however, don't be afraid to go with the long shots. Live life to its fullest every moment and be ready!

"He spoke, and there came swarms of flies, and lice in all their territory." (Psalms 105:31)

DON'T IT BUG YA?

Have you ever wanted to scratch but knew you shouldn't? Frustrating sensation, isn't it? Now I'm not talking about your average run of the mill itch that needs a good ole fashioned, door-jam rubbing. I'm referring to a serious major league creepy, crawly, mangy sensation that just won't quit.

When we went to Camp Tallaha (Boy Scout summer camp/Camp Chigger) the other day to get ready for scout camp, I forgot to take along my insect repellent. Knowing how the redbugs (chiggers) attack any un-protected skin with a vengeance, I should have been prepared, but I wasn't. "Maybe they won't be so bad this year," I wishfully dreamed. WRONG!

Even after a good hot shower that afternoon, the little beggars held on. I had no inkling of their malicious meanderings around my ankles, behind my knees, and around my waist until some 24 hours later.

At first, the sensation was only a mild titillation. With just a little concentration on other matters, I was able to ignore the urge to reach down and scratch my ankle. A few hours later, I was rummaging through the medicine cabinet for some sort of lotion, ointment, or other medicinal ministration.

By the time I located the rubbing alcohol, the home remedy suggested by one of my deacons came to mind. While in the National Guard, he had been approached by several redbug infested recruits about what to do for the terrible itching. He had instructed them to get an old rag, soak it in gasoline, scratch the chigger bites real good, and then apply the gas.

Prior to that evening, no soldier had ever managed mach .5 in a tight holding pattern without the aid of an Apache Attack Helicopter. Some of the units at not-so-nearby Ft. Payne, Alabama thought a Civil War re-enactment group was practicing for battle.

Next morning, the three chiggerless troops returned to thank the sarge. "Did it do the job?" he asked with an air of apparent concern, trying hard not to laugh in the faces of these painfully relieved recruits.

"Yes sir, Sarge. That sho' did git rid of them chiggers, but the cure was near 'bout as bad as the disease."

Well sir, like I said, after applying the rubbing alcohol to the bites I had unconsciously scratched rather thoroughly, I decided I better seek professional advice. Down at the local drug store, the prescribed cure was a small bottle with the promise of "fast relief for chigger, tick and mosquito bites" right there on the label.

Only one drop of this wonder drug promised relief. Sure enough, just about one minute after the first application, I had this not-so-subtle burning sensation. Felt kind of like certain body parts had come in contact with Mt. St. Helens at the height of the last major eruption. But it worked! After another ten minutes or so, the itching subsided, the burning cooled down, and I was busy at work typing these very words.

The Bible promises, "All things work together for good for those who love God and are called according to His purpose." That's Romans 8:28 for those of you interested in looking it up. Just think. I forgot to spray my ankles for red bugs and ticks when I went to Tallaha. The consequences were just as you would expect. The invisible varmints ate me up! But not to worry. The Lord brought something good out of this bad situation. He gave me the idea for this chapter.

Maybe the thought of putting chiggers and the Lord together in a book really bugs you. It might even tick you off.

Putting up with flies, fleas, redbugs, and these punderful chapters may be a long shot for you, but...

Whatever you do, don't be afraid to go with the long shots. Live life to its fullest every moment and be ready!

"All we, like sheep have gone astray; we have turned every one to his own way; and the Lord has laid on Him the iniquity of us all."
(Isaiah 53:6)

THE 4-H EXPERIENCE

Isn't it amazing what we're willing to do for our children? Whether it's summer baseball, Boy Scouts, or 4-H, we parents go to great lengths to provide learning opportunities for our offspring.

Sometimes I wonder who we're doing it for, though. Are we really doing it for them, or are we doing it because we missed something when we were growing up?

For the sake of the moment and the possible altruistic motives of most parents, let's just say that we're doing it for their good.

Thanks to the generosity of some mighty fine folks in our church, our three daughters have been given the opportunity over the past several years of participating in 4-H sheep showing. They went into this endeavor with parental reassurance that they would learn valuable lessons for life while working with their sheep.

Being a preacher, I figured that I could learn a few new lessons about sheep myself. After all, the Bible does say that we are all like sheep, the Lord being our Shepherd.

Well sir, I learned first hand that 4-H is a family experience, which is very, very good. It took all hands on deck to work with

24

our sheep. We had daily romps with our precious little lambs resisting the halter they were tethered to, which they obviously didn't care much for (neither the sheep nor the children)! At the end of each day came the time to feed, hay, water, and doctor the critters.

Much of what I had read and heard about sheep proved to be absolutely true. For example they're not very smart creatures. If one of them decides to run, they all run and in whatever direction the leader happens to take.

Sheep are mighty stubborn as well. One large Dorset would plant all four fickle feet firmly in the gravel on the fishpond levee and give you a look that said, "Make me walk with you if you can."

Just when thoughts of slaughter began to emerge from the recesses of my mind, and when the would-be showman (generic term indicating either male or female) was perfectly situated directly in front of the afore-mentioned hard-headed, cloven-hoofed, son of a carpet-headed — sheep, he would lunge forward like a rodeo bronc. With head down, neck bowed, and all 115 pounds of mutton streaking through the air, he would attempt to butt whomever was pulling on that infernal halter. Man, woman, or child — made absolutely no difference to him; he was bent on dealing out bumps and bruises.

At the district livestock show, one daughter was dragged around the ring by a mule-headed leg of lamb. Embarrassing — to me because the thing ran around and then walked up to me with a silly grin on her face. "Ha, now everybody knows who's responsible for my miscreant behavior."

Having addressed that dilemma before moving on to the Dixie National Jr. Round-up in Jackson the following week, I walked into the crowded show ring confident that we would not be put to shame this go round. Not so. On this occasion, the already not-too-popular Dorset decided a few laps around the show ring in front of hundreds of amused on-lookers would be appropriate.

As if "Will of the Wick" had taken lessons from his female counterpart and star of the district show, he ran away from the eldest daughter, eluded the ringmaster, his assistant, and every

County Agent present, then nonchalantly sauntered up to me and stopped. As I glared down into those big old eyes, I could read his mind, "Ha, now everybody knows . . ."

I attempted to whistle and act as though I didn't notice the large white, rag-headed sheep standing directly in front of me. Standing there in the midst of a crowd of 30-40 other dads, everything was going as planned until a fellow who **used** to be a friend of mine yelled out, "Hey, Richard, ain't that one of your sheep?"

Like I said, 4-H is a family experience. We've all learned a great deal about sheep and ourselves in the past few years. I've found out that my experiences as a pastor dealing with wayward sheep was on the money. Being a shepherd ain't all that easy!

Not many people want to be shepherds any more, and I guess I can understand why a lot better these days. You might even go so far as to say that becoming a shepherd of lost sheep is a long shot, but...

Whatever you do, don't be afraid to go with the long shots. Live life to its fullest every moment and be ready!

"Blow the trumpet in Zion, and sound an alarm in My holy mountain! Let all the inhabitants tremble; for the day of the Lord is coming." (Joel 2:1)

ALARMING, AIN'T IT?

Alarming, ain't it? The way the world is going, I mean. Lots of things are causing alarm these days — crime, inflation, too little or too much rain, earthquakes, no turkey in the freezer after many hard hunts. Life's alarming, ain't it?

Well, the other morning, I struggled through the cobwebs of my sleepy head and the grungy taste of morning breath and into my camo clothes for a turkey hunt. At 4:00 a.m. most of the world was still fast asleep as I drove through the silent streets of my hometown headed for the dark forest.

Exchanging tennis shoes for snake boots, I began to gather the junk necessary for a successful turkey hunt. Man alive, it takes a truck load of "stuff" to pull off a turkey excursion.

The coat I slipped into contained six calls, five shotgun shells, a headnet, a pair of gloves, a compass, and a couple of peppermint candies (for the breath, remember?). The fanny pack held more peppermints (really bad breath), a first-aid kit, a piece of string, some blaze orange survey tape, more turkey calls, and a small bottle of water.

Next, came the quintessential seat, a boat trailer tire tube which was made famous by <u>Tired Tubes</u>. A Forest Service employee I happened upon one day asked me why I was carrying that tube around on a turkey hunt. I told him that I could sit on the tube whenever I got tired. Would have told him about my first book, but I had other things on my mind besides explaining some of the crazy things turkey hunters do besides get up at 4:00 in the morning.

The decoy, Henrietta, hung from one shoulder, my shotgun from the other. With hat on head and flashlight in hand, I struggled to gain my feet. Finally, I sort of rolled out of the truck and headed for the most likely spot to hear a roosting turkey. Tipping silently down a badly washed-out logging road and easing across a sagebrush field, I paused on the high bank of a quiet, meandering creek. After taking a moment to catch my breath, I issued the first summons of the morning.

From somewhere far up the creek came the response of a great horned owl. (It's a thrill to speak the language!) Once again I poured forth my imitation of the owl's, "Good morning world!" Again the response came rolling back down the creek, but this time the response was that of a mature turkey gobbler. His thundering response clearly meant, "Hey, buddy, how 'bout holding it down? It's still early!"

Once more I issued the call, and again the turkey answered. I eased through the cane thicket between me and the gobbling bird to within a hundred yards of his roost tree. Sliding silently down on my tire tube next to a huge beech tree, I set up shop. "This is gonna be great," I mused as I began to break out the calls and other necessities. Softly I began to yelp like a hen on the roost, and the old boy really got worked up. He double and triple gobbled at what he thought was a new female in his area.

When sufficient light brushed aside the darkness, I cackled and gave my best impression of a hen flying down from the limb. Again, the gobbler lustily responded. I began a series of yelps, cackles, cuts, and such. The combination did the trick.

The huge bird (twenty-one pounds), sporting an eleven inch beard and inch and a half spurs, materialized out of the early morning mist. The tremendous sultan of turkeydom literally flew into my lap. I mean, before I could raise my shotgun, the turkey had crashed through the over-hanging limbs and landed only a few yards in front of me. He rolled a somersault and stood up before me, eyeball to eyeball!

At that very instant, something alarming happened. The volume was wide open. It was the clock radio in our bedroom!

Wow! What a dream! Alarming, ain't it? What preacher/

outdoor writers will do to their readers, I mean.

If trusting anything you read from this point on is going to be a long shot for you, then . . .

Whatever you do, don't be afraid to go with the long shots. Live life to its fullest every moment and be ready.

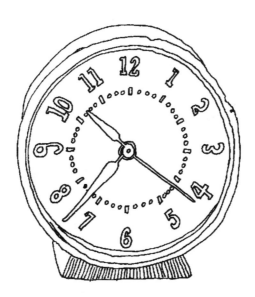

"Simon Peter said to them, `I am going fishing.' They said to him, `We are going with you also.' They went out and immediately got into the boat, and that night they caught nothing. But when the morning had now come, Jesus stood on the shore; yet the disciples did not know that it was Jesus. Then Jesus said to them, 'Children, have you any food?' They answered, 'No.' And He said to them, 'Cast the net on the right side of the boat, and you will find some.' So they cast, and now they were not able to draw it in because of the multitude of fish. Therefore, that disciple whom Jesus loved said to Peter, 'It is the Lord!' Now when Simon Peter heard that it was the Lord, he put on his outer garment (for he had removed it), and plunged into the sea. But the other disciples came in the little boat (for they were not far from land, but about two hundred cubits), dragging the net with fish. Then, as soon as they had come to land, they saw a fire of coals there, and fish laid on it, and bread. Jesus said to them, 'Bring some of the fish which you have just caught.'" (John 21:3-10)

THERE'S NOTHING LIKE IT

Ask a sky diver, and he'll tell you that there's nothing like it. There's nothing like the rush of adrenaline when you jump out of a perfectly fine airplane at 5,000 feet, or so I'm told. Likewise, there's nothing like bungy jumping. There's nothing like the emotion, the sensation of stepping off a very high object and free-falling several hundred feet toward terra firma with nothing but a very elastic piece of cord between your brains and the ground, or so I'm told.

Actually, there might possibly be one other experience like

jumping from an airplane or bungy jumping. Filling out admission papers for the nearest mental facility might come close, or so I'm told. Seriously, I think, let's get down to some sure enough "There's nothing like it" experiences. Examples? Why sure!

There's nothing like the excitement of a crappie pole bent double or a cork (for you traditional fisherpeople) doing the crappie version of a submarine's crash dive. There's nothing like it, or so I'm told.

There's nothing like the anticipation that builds and builds and builds as you watch a cork bobbing about like the staccato notes in a Spanish song because of a huge, wet-your-partner-from-one-end-of-the-boat-to-the-other bream. No, there's nothing like watching the same cork a bit later dipping and diving and heading south behind a bottom-bound bluegill. There's nothing like it, or so I'm told.

There's nothing like the spectacular splash or the dazzling dance of a seven-pound Florida bass as it consumes your jig and pig and then fights frantically to rid itself of the tasteless treat. There's nothing like it, or so I'm told.

There's nothing like the thrill of any size or type fish striking your homemade or store-bought fly. There's nothing like the singing of the leader and line followed by the groaning of a genuine bamboo or fiberglass fly rod, or so I'm told.

There's nothing like the feeling you get when you realize that a beautiful largemouth bass just sucked up your ten-inch worm and is, at that very moment, on the verge of testing the setting on your drag. Too much and — pow! Your fish is gone and with it, hook, line, and sinker, so to speak. Too little and your line reels off so fast that it smokes. In horror and helplessness you watch as you hear — pow! Your fish is gone and with it, hook, line, and sinker — again! There's nothing like it, or so I'm told.

I guess by now you've realized that I'm actually "fishing" for an invitation to experience any one or all of the above-mentioned "There's nothing like it" experiences. I do realize that this angle may be a long shot. It might even fin—ish me off, but hopefully not before it "nets" me a fishing trip or two!

Even if taking a fishing trip with one of my readers proves

to be a long shot...

Remember now, whatever you do, don't be afraid to go with the long shots. Live life to its fullest every moment and be ready!

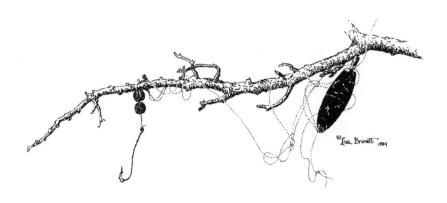

"Moreover the Lord your God will send the hornet among them until those who are left, who hide themselves from you, are destroyed." (Deuteronomy 7:20)

FLYING FIENDS

When Mr. Red Wasp tried to pierce my youngest daughter's (Lindsay) ear the other day, I was reminded of many presently painful but ultimately humorous encounters with the flying tigers of the bee family.

Here in the Deep South, we are blessed with wasps, bees, hornets, and a few other yet-to-be-named stinging insects. For the most part, these creatures of God's making mind their own business, but when we homo sapiens inadvertently infringe on their territory, they let us know in clear terms that we are definitely out of bounds and in trouble.

Years ago while performing my yard chores as a dutiful son, I ran over a yellow jacket nest with the lawnmower. This small insect carries a very painful venom in its posterior and tends to be rather irritable, especially if somebody interrupts their home building project. I suppose if I were a yellow jacket, I wouldn't appreciate being run over with a large machine that acts like a huge vacuum on my house.

I never realized I had put the giant suction to their nest until the little suckers started working on my legs. Let me tell you, folks, it's absolutely immoral what an angry swarm of yellow jackets can do to a red-headed, bermuda shorts-wearing, 15-year old. Before I knew what was going on, I had several furious stinging critters up both britches' legs. Others were threatening vital areas around my head and arms. About the second pop in the posterior, the race was on.

If I hadn't been hidden behind the house, passing motorists would have concluded, no doubt, that I was some sort of pervert or perhaps planning to audition for the part of Ray Stevens in his video "The Streak." There was no room for modesty here. The clothes had to come off, because the yellow jackets were making

33

their point quite clear.

A bath in Clorox with the resulting loss of human companionship for days eased the pain and cured the swelling, but other encounters were yet to come.

Not only do yellow jackets, hornets, and wasps initiate painful encounters of the disturbed kind, but we have a tiny little fellow who appears out of nowhere in the fall of the year to reek havoc on unsuspecting hunters.

Sitting in my tree stand one lazy October afternoon, the peace and tranquility of the moment was suddenly shattered by a piercing pain on the back of my hand. Without regard to the fact that sudden movements on a deer stand can ruin a successful hunt, I jerked my head around and raised my hand so that eyes and hand met quickly. Though my hand was stinging like fire, I couldn't see anything which might have caused the intense burning sensation.

Almost as quickly as the pain had started, it was gone. Back to the hunt, I forgot about the unexplained interruption until another hit me. Just like the first time, I couldn't determine the cause. Then, upon closer examination, I found the culprit. About the size of a straight pin point, there he was. The little devil was so tiny, but what viciousness! I watched in amazement as the midget insect opened his mouth. Would you believe it? Six-inch teeth came folding out like Edward Scissor Hands and WHAM! He bit me again.

Though I've managed to squish a few, I've yet to capture one for examination. Without a doubt, it would take a photon microscope to see the monster. If a bumble bee or hornet packed the punch per ounce of that thing, we'd all be couch potatoes! Flying fiends come in all sizes and shapes.

My good friend, Dick Taylor, from Tunica (just south of Memphis) tells about a more traditional and well-known form of flying fiends, a swarm of honey bees. Dick farms near the Splash, the first casino built along the Mississippi River in our state.

One particular spring, when it was too warm for the heater and too cool for the air conditioner, Dick had two tractors working on a soybean field. Both tractor drivers had the windows open on the big John Deeres. One tractor was discing, putting out Treflan, and the second was following, incorporating the chemical with another disc when a swarm of bees decided to invade the first tractor.

Actually, the bees were rather docile at first. Though there were hundreds of honey bees, they didn't sting the driver. But, being nervous about their presence in such close quarters, he stopped and sprayed the inside of the cab with a fire extinguisher. The foam did the trick, and the bees were anesthetized — temporarily.

Because the cab was now filled with foam, the two drivers decided to take the tractor to headquarters to wash it out. For some unknown reason, they both got into the infested tractor.

About half-way to the shop, the stunned bees came back to life. No longer docile, the bees began to reek havoc on the two men. A quick evacuation was called for, but the call went un-answered as the two fought over who would get out first.

The door wasn't wide enough to accommodate both men's exit at the same time. Each time one would nearly escape the bees' onslaught, the other would catch him and pull him back in, trying all the while to quickly take his place.

By the time the two managed to escape, the bees were finished anyway. There wasn't a stinger left in one honey bee when the swelling bodies finally got free from the den of pain. Both recovered from their stings but learned a very important lesson. Fire extinguishers will temporarily stun but definitely not kill bees, wasps, or hornets.

One summer, while working with a grass-cutting crew on Ross Barnett Reservoir near Jackson, I had the job of servicing four tractors. Mainly, my tasks included fueling up and checking the oil. "Where is that dip stick?" I'd ask, and some smart soul would holler back, "Look in the mirror!"

A mechanic I'm not, but it was my lot to change the blades on the bushhogs and bat wings (a triple section cutter on which the outside wings fold up for transfer from one place to another) and fix flats. Our four tractors consisted of a Massey Fergusson, a Ford, an International, and an old Moline.

Though I yearned to be promoted to tractor driver, I

remained chief flunky that I was. I longed to terrorize grass and weeds, but the swing blade was a safer piece of equipment with me at the helm.

One extremely hot July afternoon, the crew was cutting the right of way on a long sweeping curve when one of the bushhog drivers ran over a bumble bee nest. The crew foreman looked up in time to see the driver suddenly abandon ship as the tractor just kept on going to the bottom of the hill.

Stopping his own tractor to await the oncoming driver-less tractor, he had unknowingly placed himself in an unenviable position. The angry bees decided to take their frustration out on anything and everything that sounded like the monster that had run over their home. Whirling his tractor around in the middle of the paved road, the Massey Fergusson suddenly jumped into high gear. A second later the boss flew past me, waving his cowboy hat around like a rodeo bronc rider, screaming something I couldn't quite make out. Then he lost the grip on his hat.

As I reached down to pick up his hat, I suddenly became a lip reader. The horror of what he had said hit me nearly as hard as the punch from that bumble bee. "BUMMMM-BLE BEEEE-ES!" he was yelling. After the second one plastered me up side the head, I took off like Bo Jackson. The rest of the crew was stopped in a safe spot about a quarter mile down the road. Now, I'm not sure what the world record for the quarter mile is, but I'm quite certain that I nearly set a new one that afternoon. Some Red Man chewing tobacco and a couple of days later, I was as good as new — and a whole bunch wiser in reference to bumble bees.

There are several more good stories about flying perpetuators of pain, but I'll stop here and let you think about your own experiences. Avoiding bees, wasps, and hornets during a hot summer may be a long shot for you too, but...

Whatever you do, don't be afraid to go with the long shots. Live life to its fullest every moment and be ready!

"Do not be afraid, you beasts of the field; for the open pastures are springing up, and the tree bears its fruit; the fig tree and the vine yield their strength." (Joel 2:22)

SPRING SPORTS

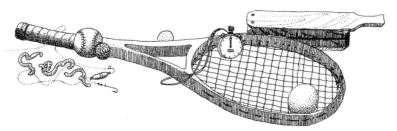

Isn't spring a wonderful time of year? As the sun's golden rays cause temperatures to climb, nearly everybody warms up to the idea of getting outside for all kinds of activities. Even the grumpiest among us have a slight twinge of good feelings when spring finally arrives.

Rising sap in the trees beckons many an outdoorsman to get out of the house and into great American spring sports. We have so many wonderful activities to choose from.

Baseball, turkey hunting, track, turkey hunting, tennis, turkey hunting, fishing, turkey hunting, farming, turkey hunting, golfing, and of course, turkey hunting are just a few outdoor activities enjoyed by many of us this time of year.

Baseball—now there's an outdoor activity(except for the domes, of course) that's in the genes of most red-blooded American youth, both male and female.

When I was nine, my Little League coach subscribed to the philosophy that Little Leaguers best learn to field ground balls by getting hit as many times and in as many different spots on their anatomy as possible. Thus would one learn what the glove is for!

In my case, however, the coach was more impressed with the amount of blood I could lose and still keep trying to stop the screaming sphere—that blinding blur that some claimed was a baseball. My definition of "hits" in the early going was not the usual.

Mercifully for me, my parents, and the coach, I moved on to track. But, woe is me, it didn't last too long either. Being small isn't an obstacle in track like it is in football or basketball—unless you're also slow, which I was and am again now that I'm past forty. Instead of using a stop watch to time me in the hundred-year dash, the coaches had to use a sun dial!

When I was relegated to the cross-country squad, I decided track was not my spring sport either. I figured this out when I discovered there was no cross-country team at dear ole Brandon High.

Bloodied and embarrassed, I pressed on to tennis. I spent days and days practicing my serve. Finally, I got the ball toss down pretty good and asked, "Mom, can I have a racket now?" With 22.5 books of green stamps, she purchased my first tennis racket, a Don Budge wooden job—with strings.

Hundreds of serves daily wore the hide off the used tennis balls I found around the edges of our local court. With confidence running high, I gave my buddy down the street, James King, a call. "Wanna play some tennis this afternoon?"

"Didn't know you knew how."

"I've been practicing."

We met at center court of the asphalt-surfaced public tennis court in Brandon, Mississippi at tea time. James said, "You serve first." So I did.

"You're supposed to hit the ball over the net first, dip stick! This ain't ping pong."

So it was that I served a very short stint at tennis and moved on to other, more noble and time-honored spring sports, fishing and farming.

Now, I realize that some folks might not see the vital link between fishing and farming, but they do go hand in hand. My father always thought that Saturday was for working around the yard or in the garden. At first, the very idea of working in the garden on a perfectly beautiful spring day was outrageous. In case all my friends called wanting to know if I wanted to go fishing or something, I'd practice breathing out a long, slow, pitiful sigh of anguish and say, "Naw, I can't. I gotta work in the garden today."

I never had to use the line, but it would have come in handy if someone invited me to go fishing. I'd have at least one line, don't you see?

Those Saturdays could have continued to be frustrating and ulcer-producing, but I learned that farming and fishing could compliment one another. There's always something good in the worst of situations. Plowing beans or breaking the garden for the first time always yielded lots of long, juicy, fish-attracting earth-worms. By the time I got through plowing or hoeing, I'd have more bait than Sonny or I either one needed to go catch a sack full of big old bream. If the yard needed mowing, well sir, the crickets were usually as thick as fleas on my dog's back. More bait, don't you see?

About the time I turned fifteen, both fishing and farming were getting to be old hat. Kid's stuff to the mature adolescent. It was time to set aside the fishing pole and the bean poles. The gentleman's game of golf was beckoning.

Somebody told me that you **play** baseball and tennis, **run** track, **do** yard work, **go** fishing, but you **shoot** golfs. Since I was beginning to cultivate an interest in hunting, I naively assumed that golf would be my spring sport for sure.

I dreamed of shooting birdies, real trophies, but discovered that my skills weren't up to par! (Well, at least I had the language of the links down pat) Far be it from me to shoot an Eagle, a federal offense, don't you know? My intense interest in old war movies, especially about the Army Air Corps, perfectly prepared me for the bogeys that began flying my way, especially the double, triple, and quadruple bogeys.

My friend and classmate—now surgeon—Buddy Puckett, explained, "One more than par is bogey. Two more is double bogey, but for the life of me, I don't know how to describe what your score is after the first hole. Phenomenal is about as accurate as I can get."

Thrilled with such an exciting compliment, I broke out in a wide grin. Shoot, I didn't know that the lower the score the better. I thought shooting golfs was like all other sports I had participated in (loosely speaking, of course). Golf is the only spring sport I know of where the fewer the points the better.

Finally, after thirty something springs, I discovered the ultimate spring sport. Thus I moved on, which is what I need to do right now. Turkey hunting, anyone?

Finding a spring sport that suits you as much as turkey hunting suits me may be a long shot for you, but...

Whatever you do, don't be afraid to go with the long shots. Live life to the fullest every moment and be ready!

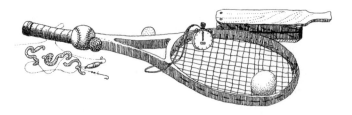

"But if a woman has long hair, it is a glory to her; for her hair is given to her for a covering."(I Corinthians 11:15)

MR. BOB

Paper sacks have many uses. Not only do they bring home the bacon from the grocery store, they perform many other useful tasks. They help gather up the trash around the house, and when paper towels are in short supply, they make a fair drain for french fries.

Growing up in Brandon in the early 60's, my next door neighbor was the retired County Agent, Mr. Bob Prescott. Mr. Bob was the best neighbor a young boy could have. He took me fishing for bream, and he knew where every bream bed in the county was and when they'd be biting the best. According to Mr. Bob, the answer to, "Where did ya'll catch them pretty breams?" was always, "In the mouth!"

Mr. Bob's first wife had died several years earlier. It was a real sad time around that part of Jasper Street, but after a while, we noticed that Mr. Bob had a new car. That was mighty strange. In 1960, he was still driving his 1950 Chevrolet pick-up. Obviously, he'd gone and gotten his priorities out of whack.

Anyhow, not only did Mr. Bob buy a new car, but he started going off during the day quite often—in the car! To this ten-year-old novice in the matter of romance, all this didn't make a smidgen of sense.

Well sir, first thing we knew, rumor had it that Mr. Bob was courting some lady from up around Fannin, close to the Barnett Reservoir, which is near Jackson for those of you who are still trying to figure out where the place is, as if it really matters. Her name was Miss Stella, and she was supposed to be a real catch for the widower/retired county agent/fisherman. I thought so too when I found out she liked to fish!

The day they got hitched, Mr. Bob didn't tell a soul, except the preacher of course. He was real secretive about the whole thing. "How secretive was he?" you ask. (I knew you'd ask.)

Mr. Bob was so secretive that he put the proverbial paper

41

sack to a totally new and heretofore unheard of use. When they got close enough to town for someone to recognize Miss Stella, he had her put a grocery sack over her head!

Now folks, I've heard of people so ugly they needed a sack over their head, but this just wasn't true of Miss Stella. Even to a ten-year-old, and her about sixty, she was a nice lookin' lady. According to the groom, he just didn't want all the old busy-bodies in Brandon knowing his business.

Thinking back on that use of a grocery sack was stirred by an even stranger use of the widely recognized brown bag. Out in the hills where some of us deer hunt these days, lives a gentleman named Milton. Milton cuts a little pulpwood, pittles a might, enjoys a good rabbit hunt and a snort now and then.

Like so many of us dog lovers, Milton has a favorite dog. It's a one-eyed beagle hound. Used to be every time Milton left his trailerhouse to drive into Lexington, the hound would chase after the truck just a'barking until Milton would finally have to stop and pick him up.

After a while, Milton learned to load up the dog to begin with rather than have to stop on the way. Nowadays, Ole Cyclops just sits there on the seat of Milton's truck like he belongs, one paw propped up on the door like he's Mr. Cool.

The only problem Milton had when he initiated this arrangement was that the dog just wouldn't stop barking from the time they left until they got back home. Since the beagle can't see out of his right eye, he must've figured that there's always another dog lurking out there on his blind side. Naturally, the only thing to do in that situation is bark.

As you can imagine, the incessant barking got old quick, so Milton resorted to ingenuity. He got a grocery sack and stuck it on the dog's head so he couldn't see, reasoning that if he couldn't see anything, he wouldn't bark. Strange reasoning, I know, but that's Milton.

The maiden voyage of the sack cruise came by our camp and, as usual, Milton stopped to speak. Though it's only a quarter mile from his house to our camp, the hound had already chewed a hole in the sack. There was Milton grinning and the dog barking, his nose and mouth protruding from the Sunflower sack! A barking grocery bag isn't an every day sight.

Puttin' your grocery sacks to such whimsical uses may be a long shot for you, but...

Whatever you do, don't be afraid to go with the long shots. Live life to its fullest every moment and be ready!

"I watch, and am as a sparrow alone upon the housetop."
(Psalms 102:7)

BIRD WATCHING

What image comes to mind when you think of a bird watcher? I don't know about you, but I conjure up a British gentleman in a tweed suit, derby hat, walking cane, mustache, greying hair, one of those funny-looking stools, and a pair of small binoculars.

As a young person, I thought the only people who sat around watching birds were old folks and members of the Audubon Society. In my narrow world of experience, the latter were rather strange people who didn't believe in eating meat or hunting, things normal people do, don't you see?

Anyhow, the times must be changing. These days there's a bird feeder hanging in our backyard and a pair of binoculars always handy. Can you believe it? We're talking about a hunting devotee here, watching birds!

If you don't have a bird feeder in your backyard, then you don't know what you're missing. It really is a thrill to watch a couple dozen house sparrows, a pair of blackbirds, a rockin' robin, and a mourning dove or two flitting in the yard.

For someone who has hunted doves for thirty-plus years, I can't believe it myself. I'm actually enjoying watching the grey darters feeding, playing, and preening themselves. One of my favorite games is to imitate their calls and watch them cock their head this way and that, trying to figure out where their compadre is. The shock is evident when they finally realize that the song is coming from a human relaxing in a lounge chair!

Mockingbirds are another fascination. They are so cocky, obnoxious and worrisome as well. They mock the songs of other birds, which is aggravating to say the least. Cats and squirrels

44

beware as well! A mockingbird will attack without warning like a German Stuka dive bomber.

Blue jays are also annoying to the other birds. They seem to delight in scolding others, and they don't cut squirrels any slack either. When one finds something to worry, he starts calling all the others in the neighborhood. Soon they have a cacophony of cries ringing out, announcing to the world that they're giving some poor critter the business.

Rockin' robin is another story. He minds his own business, and obviously has plenty of it to mind. Preferring to run here and there rather than fly, the robin is constantly on the lookout for earthworms. His keen eyesight and constant vigilance mean that worms better keep their heads down or lose them. After a rain, when worms come to the surface to avoid being drowned, the robins have a heyday.

It's absolutely amazing to me, but the most thrilling topic of conversation with the neighbors these days concerns birds. One neighbor has a host of purple martins, which is not only entertaining, but also helps keep down the mosquito population.

A red-headed woodpecker started showing up at the neighbor's feeder a while back. While the other birds are busy picking up spilled seed or munching away on the feeder, Woody the Woodpecker works on one of several pine stumps nearby.

I'm still amazed that I get as excited as I do about the appearance of certain birds. The beautiful goldfinch that suddenly showed up one afternoon was as thrilling as the hummingbird that nearly sat on my head one morning when I was turkey hunting. And astonishingly beautiful is the only way to describe the cardinal.

The Good Lord sure has put some mighty fine looking feathery friends in our world. They all have a purpose, you know, an important place in the scheme of things. I happen to think that one of their reasons for being is our enjoyment.

The pleasure of bird watching seems to be catching on. Because bird watching is such pleasure, bird feeders and bird baths are cropping up all over town these days. No doubt, some of our more fiercely dedicated hunters will think all this talk about bird watching is for the . . .

Okay, I didn't say it. For once, I stopped before I got wound up with the puns. All the groans from the reading audience are just about to take the pun out of writing this tale. Oops!

Putting up with my puns and bird watching may be long shots for you, but...

Whatever you do, don't be afraid to go with the long shots. Live life to its fullest every moment and be ready!

"Now Solomon's provision for one day was thirty kors of fine flour, sixty kors of meat, ten fatted oxen, twenty oxen from the pastures, and one hundred sheep, besides deer, gazelles, roebucks, and fatted fowl." (I Kings 4:22-23)

DID SOMEONE CRY, "FOWL"?

What do guineas, geese, and gobblers have in common? Let me give you a hint. In times past, all these feathery fowl were found in nearly every yard out in the country. No respectable farm house went without these three sentinels of country life.

As a young boy, I remember taking a trip to visit some of our kin on my father's side of the family. They lived out in rural Hinds County, Ms. on a farm. The house was a huge "dog trot" house, poised some six feet off the ground on stone pillars. Spacious rooms with 14-foot ceilings lined the interior hallway, which ran completely through the house and opened on the back. This open hallway is what gave the name "dog trot" to this type building. The dogs could walk through the house without actually going into any of the rooms.

Each room had its own fireplace, which came in mighty handy on cold winter nights. With those high ceilings, the houses got terribly cold. The brick fireplaces were the center of attention for over-night visits in the winter. If I backed up real close to the fireplace, I could get one side toasted while the other froze. The trick was to get just warm enough without letting my pants get too hot. When my mental timer failed me and I turned around too quickly, my pants legs would make contact, and around and around I'd go trying to cool off singed flesh!

Those whirlwind circuits about the room to cool off my backside prepared me for other circuits I had to make at the old farm house. Out in the yard, unbeknownst to me, the Beasley's had

47

constructed a race track. Now, it wasn't the kind that human beings would recognize, but to the fowl in the yard, it was the perfect proving ground for attempts at setting new world land-speed records.

The first time I was introduced to the track and the need for speed, I was the last one out of the car. All the other family members had already reached the porch before I became aware of the threat. As I slowly made my way to the steps, a large goose moved into a blocking position and began to hiss at me.

In my six-year-old eyes(which were about the same height as the goose's eyes), this monster gander would go about 250 pounds! As I began to consider a strategic withdrawal, a couple of giant guinea fowl blocked my retreat in two of the remaining directions. Just as I turned to my last available avenue of departure, the boss gobbler of the entire world hit the track.

Running like the wind, I began the first lap. It's truly astounding how much dust a six-year-old and a mature gobbler, a goose, and a flock of guineas can stir up—especially when the six-year-old is churning up the ground because of a lack of traction on his worn-out tennis shoes! I looked like a cartoon character trying to get started.

When the shoe soles finally caught a root, I was off like an F-14 Tomcat. Comfortable in the thought that I had instantly reached mach 1.5 and set a new world land-speed record all at once, I was shocked to look back and discover the gobbler right behind me—nibbling at my right behind!

My family sat on the porch in awed silence. No one had ever seen such speed from moi. After the third or fourth round trip, someone finally stuck a foot out and stopped me. The dust was so thick it was beginning to irritate the family, and the gobbler had long since quit chasing me. He was settled under a big oak tree, cooling off with a long sip of well water, laughing and joking with the guineas and the goose about scarin' another youngun.

Experiencing the terror of guineas, geese, and gobblers at your family's farmhouse may be a long shot for you, but...
Whatever you do, don't be afraid to go with the long shots. Live life to its fullest every moment and be ready!

"He is despised and rejected by men, a man of sorrows and acquainted with grief. And we hid, as it were, our faces from Him; He was despised, and we did not esteem Him. Surely He has borne our griefs and carried our sorrows; yet we esteemed Him stricken, smitten by God, and afflicted. But He was wounded for our transgressions. He was bruised for our iniquities; the chastisement for our peace was upon Him, and by His stripes we are healed."

(Isaiah 53:2-5)

HIDE AND SEEK

Growing up, I was the undisputed master of hiding out in such cleverly conceived coverts that no one, including my sleuth-nosed mother, could find me. In a thoroughly exciting game of hide and seek, I did the hiding and the rest of the family did the seeking. It was great fun—for me, at least. I enjoyed our games beyond measure.

James and Mary Frances and elder brother, Sonny, didn't exactly share the thrill of the chase with me. After an hour or so of intense searching for the lost sibling, Sonny would throw his hands up and quit in disgust(sore loser!) He just didn't have a love for the game like his little brother, but Mother was another story. She would really get into the thick of it.

Mother would get her short, stocky frame and red hair, with temperament to boot, wound up in frantically seeking her lost child. She would stomp her feet and shout in mock indignation. (Surely she wasn't seriously angry with sweet little ole me, do you think?) At the appropriate moment in the game, she would yell into the emptiness of space, "When I find you, you little red-headed turkey(or some other domesticated farm animal, the type of which I can no longer recollect), I'm gonna beat you to within an inch of your short life!" Mother always did lend such a glorious sense of drama to our games with her feigned fits of wrath.

Through the years, hide and seek has taken many forms in

49

my life. I've been amazingly adept in most of these. ·

For example, Sonny tried in vain to make me mind whenever our parents were away for a few hours and we were home alone. It never worked though. Once he tried to physically restrain me, but while his back was momentarily turned, locking the door to prevent my escape, I slugged him with a baseball bat(kids, don't try this at home).

Well, as you might imagine, when he came to, I was well hidden in the best place ever. I was under the pillows on our parent's bed. How I managed to make up the bed while lying beneath the pillows still amazes me, but it worked perfectly. When Mother finally arrived home(I was nearly dead from suffocation), Sonny still hadn't located me. Perhaps he would have found me if he had stopped yelling and running all over the wood-frame house long enough to listen to the labored breathing in the master bedroom.

Then there was the time I and a few others hid from our high school choral director, Miss Polk. While this sweet lady's back was turned, working with the sopranos, us tenors and bases slipped out of the room, one by one. When she finally realized that she couldn't hear enough of the men's parts because there were no men left in the room, we had been hiding behind the curtains in the auditorium long enough to drink a coke and laugh ourselves into asthma at being so slick.

When the principal found us, we paid dearly for our foolish prank. Seeing poor Miss Polk in tears was the worst punishment we could have received. The licks weren't too pleasant either, as I recall.

Another of my glorious hiding experiences came when I hid from an angry boyfriend who was threatening to tear me apart, limb from limb. How was I to know that the girl was going steady with a guy from another town who just happened to be a blackbelt in karate? I didn't know she wanted to break up with the guy but was afraid of him. When he showed up at my house late one night as I was arriving home from a date with HIS girlfriend, I demonstrated once again my prowess at hiding.(Hey, I'm a lover, not a fighter.)

One of my better performances occurred once while I was

squirrel hunting with Sonny. He got lost and turned around something terrible. Just before going into warp panic, he turned and there I stood. Naturally, he didn't mean to(get lost to find me). If he hadn't gotten lost, he never would have found me. This was the only time I can ever remember him winning one of our games of hide and seek. "Great going, Sonny! I didn't think you would ever find me this time!"

I had gone off deep into the woods in southern Rankin County and turned around so many times trying to sneak up on some of those wily cat squirrels that I didn't think anybody would ever find me. Then Sonny popped up.

Thinking quickly, I suggested we play the game together. It was great fun, more fun than he had ever realized. We stayed hidden in the woods for hours and hours and only decided to let people find us when we realized that we had fooled them for so long that they had called off the search for the night.

As much as I hate to admit it though, I used to be very good at hiding from dirty diapers, using any and every excuse in the book to get out of the house at the most opportune times. The feint whiff of ammonia or baby powder or any other odor closely associated with small babies would send me back to the days of my youth, and off I would go in a trot to find some neat hiding place. The older I get, though, the harder it becomes to successfully hide.

On a serious note, my most successful hiding was done for years as I hid from God. I knew in my heart that He loved me and died on the cross for me, but I kept on hiding from Him. I was really stupid, because even though I couldn't see Him, He always saw me. The wonderful thing is, He still loves me in spite of all my hiding from Him. I thank Him that one day He came into my life in such a personal and real way as to help me see that I hadn't lost the game when He found me.

Hiding from God, the seeker and saver of sinners, is more than a long shot. It's a useless effort. His great love compels Him to seek for us until He finds us and offers us the gift of eternal life through faith in Jesus Christ in a way that we simply can't resist. Even if you still think being found by God and finding God in a real and personal way are long shots...

Whatever you do, don't be afraid to go with the long shots.
Live life to its fullest every moment and be ready!

"Thus says the Lord, 'A great eagle with large wings and long pinions, full of feathers of various colors, came to Lebanon and took from the cedar the highest branch." (Ezekiel 17:3)

OUR REAL NATIONAL BIRD

Benjamin Franklin, with all his diplomatic and political skills, couldn't convince the other founding fathers that the Wild Turkey should be our national bird. What did the man see in turkeys anyway? Beauty? Not hardly. A Wild Turkey is one of the ugliest critters on earth, except to another turkey, of course. Its power perhaps? Definitely not. Though it can run as fast as a deer and fly as gracefully as a dove, the turkey isn't known for its strength.

Do you want to know what I think? Well, since this is my book, I'll tell you anyway, you turkey!

I believe that wise old Ben Franklin pushed so hard for the Wild Turkey as our national bird because it is a feisty, finicky, feathery fiend. "Do what?" you cry in disbelief. You heard me right. The Wild Turkey is a feisty, finicky, feathery fiend—a description I will gladly explain to you naysayers.

From his perch high above the forest floor, a wild turkey gobbler will take on all comers in the wee hours of the morning. An owl hoots. He gobbles. A crow caws. He gobbles. A truck door slams. He gobbles. Another gobbler gobbles. He gobbles. The Good Lord thunders from his heavens, and yep, you guessed it. He gobbles. Feisty, ain't he?

"What about the finicky part?" you ask. You did ask, didn't you? I thought so.

The wild turkey gobbler, albeit feisty as he can be, is still more finicky than Morris the Cat. Chauvinistic, as well. When a hen turkey yelps, cackles, cuts, purrs, clucks, or otherwise winks in his direction, especially in the spring time, the old boy will gobble his head off(the feisty part coming out, don't you see?), but he won't come to her. He'll stand out there and gobble, drum, strut, and show off all his colors(he's pretty only during these demonstrations of male superiority).

Come to her? Not on your life! That's woman's work in the turkey world. If she thinks he's hot stuff, she can come to him,

53

thank you mam! There are just too many fine females who'll come to him for him to take chances or waste time and effort on some new-to-the-neighborhood feathery female. Finicky, ain't he?

"Feathery, I understand," you say? Granted. A turkey's feathers are special though. Perhaps there are some of the finer details about the feathery part that you don't already know. Reckon?

To begin with, did you know that there are four sub-species of Wild Turkey in North America? Sure enough!

We have the Eastern Wild Turkey down here in the Mississippi Delta part of Dixie. Florida has the Osceola, South Texas the Rio Grande, and out west, the Merriam.

Without boring you to death with details(HEY! WAKE UP FELLA! I'M TALKING TO YOU!), I'll just share a few tasty tidbits of turkey trivia about the Eastern version of the Wild Turkey. This stuff might come in handy if you try hunting these devils of the deep woods.

The turkey hen is rather drab in color and sports a bland white head. She blends in well with her environment though, which comes in real handy when she's trying to raise a family after the spring mating season. Predators abound during this time of year, looking for an easy meal of fresh turkey eggs.

The gobbler is another story when it comes to color. He looks really ugly when he's just out and about for a stroll. His head is blue, but this changes rapidly when he's confronted by another gobbler wanting to fight or by a hen looking for love in the spring. Then his head flushes with the color of brilliant red.

His tail feathers, which usually trail along behind neatly folded and drooping, suddenly stand upright and fan out like a peacock's. He's just about that proud, too! His chest swells, and every bronze-colored feather on his body seems to shine like the gold in Fort Knox.

When a hen is near, he'll make a drumming sound with the nodes on his neck, which is supposed to mean, "Hey, hey! What do you think, baby?" He'll swirl round and round like he's doing the Viennese waltz, stopping frequently to gobble and checking to see if his dance is doing the trick on the amorous hen.

54

Sitting up against a giant white oak tree, still as a church mouse, watching a feisty, finicky, feathery fella do this just out of shotgun range after a two-hour ordeal of trying to call him in with all the seduction possible, leads us to the last word on the Wild Turkey—fiend.

Late one spring turkey season, I aroused a feisty fella with an owl hoot. A friend and I raced to within a hundred yards or so of his roost and set up our trap.

We called softly at first like a hen still on the roost. The gobbler responded lustily and immediately with his distinctive gobble. A real feisty fella!

When it got light enough for the turkeys to fly down, he sailed away from us. Finicky, don't ya see? Time after time, I followed him through the woods, setting up and calling. All the way to grandmother's house we went. I'd call. He'd stop, gobble, drum, and strut, but after a while, he turned and walked away again. Finicky, a real finicky fella!

At last, I drew close and let go the sweetest, sexiest note I knew in his language. He gobbled just the other side of a little hill from me. When he didn't come on around the side of the knoll, I got up to move again, and...

Fiendish, ain't I? Guess I've been in the woods with way too many turkeys lately.

Finding out how this hunt ended will prove to be a real long shot for you, but...

Whatever you do, don't be afraid to go with the long shots. Live life to its fullest every moment, and be ready!

"Now a herd of many swine was feeding there on the mountain. And they begged Him that He would permit them to enter them. And he permitted them. Then the demons went out of the man and entered the swine, and the herd ran violently down the steep place into the lake and drowned." (Luke 8:32-33)

SUBMARINE HOG HUNT

The sport of hunting wild boar isn't for everyone. It isn't even for every hunter. Hog hunting is one of those challenges that few should or do take up, and fewer still continue after just one taste. It's easy to bite off more than you can chew in one round with a wild hog, the hog being the one doing the biting!

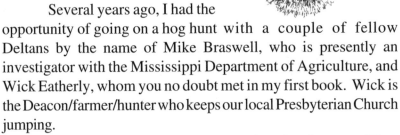

Several years ago, I had the opportunity of going on a hog hunt with a couple of fellow Deltans by the name of Mike Braswell, who is presently an investigator with the Mississippi Department of Agriculture, and Wick Eatherly, whom you no doubt met in my first book. Wick is the Deacon/farmer/hunter who keeps our local Presbyterian Church jumping.

Now folks, these two men are serious hog hunters. They have the hog dogs, horses, weapons, all the necessary equipment, and most important of all, the intense desire to chase a mad, teeth-clicking, grunting, 300-pound wild boar hog at breakneck speed through thick timber.

To tell you the truth, after the first encounter with a wild hog, I didn't think I would ever try it again, but then I've changed my mind before. So when Wick called and invited me to go hog hunting again, since no other season was open, I said, "Yes," before I even thought about what I was committing myself to. An insane asylum would have been safer!

The frequent spring rains over the previous two months had swollen every bayou and dip in the woods with water neck deep on a giraffe. The weather had finally cleared up so that we had three days of perfectly beautiful blue skies and mild temperatures.

Our first day was rather uneventful, except for one brief, exciting chase that ended with the dogs catching a small boar, which we cut and turned loose. The horse ride was sure enough a thrill! It isn't often that I get to play cowboy, hat off, hollering and spurring the horse to go wide open. It was great!

The second day I found it much more difficult to climb up on the back of my ride. Tender is the word that comes to mind as I recollect touching the saddle that morning. The first half hour was truly a painful experience. Shoot, it's still a painful memory!

The entourage made its way through the deep woods until the dogs finally struck. The race was on. Dogs, hogs, and cowboys went in nearly every direction remotely mentioned on a compass. Some of us had to pull dogs off young pigs, others from sows, and finally we got on the trail of our quarry.

A huge, spotted Russian boar hog led the dogs on a merry chase, with horses and riders in hot pursuit. The first hunter to arrive at the sight where the boar had made his stand was a rather rotund young man. He made the mistake of many a novice when he rode up close and dismounted. His intentions were honorable. He intended to quickly dispatch the raging rack of ribs before some of the dogs got cut or killed.

Instead of dispatching the hog, however, the hog busted out from among the baying hounds and made right for the hunter. The whole scene happened so quickly that Jeffrey had no time to fire his weapon. He threw down his rifle and shimmeyed up the nearest tree, which happened to be about six inches in diameter and no more than 20 feet tall. A picture of the 200-plus pound hunter no more than a couple of feet up the stressed out tree still draws huge draughts of laughter whenever a crowd of cowboy hog hunters gathers to reminisce about the heydays of wild boar hunting.

Participating in a wild boar hunt or being a real cowboy may be a long shot for you, but...

Whatever you do, don't be afraid to go with the long shots. Live life to its fullest every moment and be ready!

Jesus said, "He who receives you receives Me, and he who receives Me, receives Him who sent Me. He who receives a prophet in the name of a prophet shall receive a prophet's reward. And he who receives a righteous man in the name of a righteous man shall receive a righteous man's reward. And whoever gives one of these little ones only a cup of cold water in the name of a disciple, assuredly, I say to you, he shall by no means lose his reward."(Matthew 10:40-42)

REWARDING

Fishing with the family is a truly rewarding experience. The rewards range from, "Thanks, Dad," to "Dad, why is my hook hanging in your ear? I thought you took a dim view of men wearing earrings!"

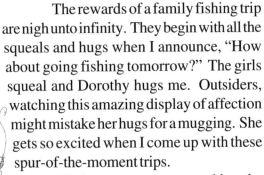

The rewards of a family fishing trip are nigh unto infinity. They begin with all the squeals and hugs when I announce, "How about going fishing tomorrow?" The girls squeal and Dorothy hugs me. Outsiders, watching this amazing display of affection might mistake her hugs for a mugging. She gets so excited when I come up with these spur-of-the-moment trips.

All the necessary stops add to the excitement. At the grocery store, we stop for ice, drinks, junk food, roll paper. (With four women, it's best to not leave home without it!) This is especially rewarding for the store owner.

Other stops include the service station for gas, a friend's house for tackle, and the bait shop. It's so rewarding to see the children and wife jumping with excitement over the trip—the trip the escaping crickets cause while making their way around the car!

Upon arriving at the lake, there are the rewards of working out a backlash on a casting reel. A true backlash looks like an old fondoo hair style, all puffed up, sticking out in every direction. Trying for hours to straighten out a rat's nest inside a casting reel yields all kinds of rewards, patience being the main most one of all.

Patience is such a hard virtue to acquire on a family outing, especially when the women keep asking, "Say, Dad, how DID you get that thing so balled up on the first cast?"

"Funny, real funny," but very rewarding!

Then there's the joy of freeing tangled lines. How can four people manage to entwine their lines so that it appears there are at least three hundred bream poles involved? Rewarding.

I am also constantly amazed at how frequently the line on a cane pole can find its way up amongst tree limbs. I reckon that explains why fresh-water flying fish seem to be extinct. Rewarding.

How about snagged hooks? Submerged objects lie in wait for a peacefully settling hook to come along. Suddenly, a benign tree top turns into a snarling snagger of barbed bream hooks. We're talking about a major rewarding experience here!

Of course, what can beat the obvious reward of a healthy jog back and forth between four females who won't bait a hook with worm, cricket, or minnow? Oh, how rewarding!

Removing fish from the hook, so that I'm the only one at the end of the day with scratched, cut, and gouged hands, is so rewarding.

Stringing fish for everyone, then discovering that a turtle or snake has been eating the catch as fast as we've been putting them on the stringer is so rewarding.

Lugging what's left of the day's catch from the pond to the cleaning rack and taking care of the yucky part is so rewarding. It doesn't bother me when I can pass along the techniques of filleting a bass or scraping the scales off a bream, but most times the women folk disappear when the moment of truth arrives. Rewarding.

Just as I stagger back into the kitchen with the cleaned fish, I hear the old familiar tune. "Hon, would you mind cooking the fish? You fry fish so much better than I do." Lordy, it's rewarding!

As you can see, the rewards are too numerous to recount. Hoping to enjoy a relaxing day fishing with a family of four females may be a long shot, but...

Whatever you do, don't be afraid to go with the long shots. Live life to its fullest every moment and be ready!

"How the mighty have fallen in the midst of the battle!"
(II Samuel 1:25a)

BOAT PADDLE GOBBLER

Spring in Mississippi is like a moody person. Some days start out warm and sunny, and by noon it's cold and raining, the wind blowing ninety to nothing right out of the north. This particular spring day be-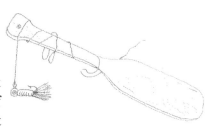gan kind of cool, but still pleasant. The fishing partners decided the crappie would be biting and had decided the night before to give in to the lure of fishing for white perch the next morning.

True to the information gleaned from listening in on private conversations in the local coffee shop the day before, the crappie were biting. The spot they heard mentioned was perfect. The color jig was right on the money, and the depth of six feet put them right in the middle of the bedding fish.

After pulling in half a limit apiece in short order, they decided to give the hot spot a rest. Another pretty place down the lake beckoned because of success there in past years. They pulled the jig poles in and lifted the trolling motor out of the water. Both men donned their life jackets and cranked the 80-horse Johnson for a quick trip down the lake.

They had only covered a few hundred yards when they rounded a bend in the ox-bow lake. To their absolute surprise, there was a full-grown turkey gobbler running down the edge of the lake.

"Look at that," Jimmy cried.

"What? Where? What is it?" the ship's captain yelled above the roar of the engine as he jerked his head around trying to pick up whatever it was that was so exciting.

"There," pointed his buddy at the near bank of the lake. At that instant, he saw it too. Sure enough, a mature turkey gobbler running like the Yankees at the first battle of Bull Run just below the bluff on the edge of the water. The ole boy looked like Bo Jackson, dipping and diving, a bronze blur.

"Turn into the bank," Jimmy cried to the helmsman.

"Do what?"

"Turn into the bank! Cut him off!"

"What're you gonna do?"

"Just turn this thing into the bank ahead of him and see."

"But you don't even have a shotgun or rifle, not even a pistol."

"Turn into the bank, I said!" the heating and cooling contractor yelled.

"Okay, okay."

The engine revved up another notch, and the pair sped by the racing turkey. Suddenly, the bow of the boat spun around, sending a cascade of water down the lake and nearly tossing the would-be gobbler-getter out of the boat.

The turkey leaped up and over the bluff and dove into a fallen tree top for cover. The paddle-wielding crappie fisherman, turned turkey hunter, raced up to the forest fortress. As he leaped on top to flush the bird, the old Tom stuck his head out to see if the way was clear for a dash to freedom. Only problem was, the spot he chose to take a peek was within reach of the paddle.

Yep, you guessed it. With one perfectly placed lick, the huge gobbler was history. The incredible potentate of turkeydom sported a ten-inch beard and a fine set of spurs.

"Incredible," some will conclude. "Unbelievable," others will say. "Come on now, you expect me to believe this?" you ask.

Well, it's like Dizzy Dean used to say about bragging. "It ain't braggin', if you done it," and on Easter Sunday in the sanctuary of the local Methodist Church, before God and the entire congregation, Donahoo swore that he done it!

Taking a trophy turkey with a boat paddle is a long shot for sure, but...

Whatever you do, don't be afraid to go with the long shots. Live life to its fullest every moment and be ready!

"Then the daughter of Pharaoh came down to wash herself at the river. And her maidens walked along the river's side; and when she saw the ark among the reeds, she sent her maid to get it."

(Exodus 2:5)

Queen of the Nile

Moonbeams reflected off the glassy waters of the River Nile performing like theater spotlights, illuminating the balcony of our room at the Oberoi Aswan. Situated on the beautiful Elaphatine Island near Aswan in southern Egypt, this tropical paradise captivated all five senses at once. Every nerve ending detected the myriad of nuances of the night, soaking up cultural spills like a sponge.

The quiet of the midnight hour which beckoned me was occasionally broken by traffic on the distant city streets. The faint sound of an Egyptian band performing local music with a distinctive beat wasn't the least bit out of place or distracting in the peaceful evening air.

Palm trees waved gently in the cool night breeze, greeting my arrival on the terrace with typical native warmth. A bat suddenly swooped down, dipping himself in the pale aura of the pool-side lights, departing as quickly into the inky darkness as he had appeared.

Somewhere out in the western darkness lay the vast Sahara Desert. The foreboding sand dunes stopped a mere hundred yards from the river's bank. A sailboat slipped by in the murky waters, providing the newlyweds with a romantic memory of their Egyptian honeymoon.

As I walked back into the room and switched off the remaining light, the sudden shroud of darkness(so deep I could feel and hear it) made me think of a saying my mother often used on especially dark nights. "It's as dark as Egypt," I thought to myself and then laughed. It was Egypt!

Waking just at sunrise the next morning, the trance which had overwhelmed me hours earlier with its beauty and tranquility, yielded still further displays of Egyptian elegance. The Saharan sand dunes, at the first light of day, were as red as a fire engine. A freshening breeze and a powder blue sky followed on the heels of the rising golden orb.

Doves cooed. Crows cawed. A thousand egrets eloped in the palm trees on the western shore. I sat and attempted to take in the panorama, as sparrows stopped by frequently checking out the new guests, obviously looking for a hand-out.

The waters of the Nile flow northward to the Mediterranean Sea. Thus when we flew south, we were actually going up river. The Nile in upper(southern) Egypt is as blue as azure. The feluccas(sailboats) which are found up and down the Nile come in all sizes and serve as ferries in the nearly total absence of bridges.

In southern Egypt, far from the colossal crowds and aggravating hucksters of Cairo, people are warm and friendly. Service aboard our Oberoi tour ship was impeccable. It seemed as though five to ten people were constantly available to meet the slightest whim of each of us on the cruise. These cordial gentlemen spoke English better than some Americans I know.

For those of you interested in an Egyptian holiday, I'd strongly recommend a day or two in Cairo to see the important sites. You need to see the pyramids in nearby Giza, the step pyramid of Sakarra, the papyrus and carpet mills, and especially the King Tut exhibit in the Egyptian Museum. Then fly on to Aswan and cruise the Nile in comfort for three or four days, enjoying the attention of the gracious crew and soaking up the sights and sounds of 5,000 years of Egyptian history. It will be a trip you'll never forget.

Taking such a trip to the Middle East, except in your imagination, may be a long shot for you, but...

Whatever you do, don't be afraid to go with the long shots. Live life to its fullest every moment and be ready!

In the heat of summer

"And the Lord spoke to Moses, 'Go to Pharaoh and say to him, "Thus says the Lord: Let My people go, that they may serve Me." But if you refuse to let them go, behold, I will smite all your territory with frogs.'"(Exodus 8:1-2)

IF A FROG HAD WINGS

For a hunter, the months of June, July, and August can be mighty depressing. The only season open is frog hunting, which unlike Egypt's problems with the cold-blooded critters just prior to Israel's exodus, has some tasty rewards for those brave enough to fight the mosquitos and the snakes to capture a cooler full. Fried frog legs are about as good a meal as this writer can imagine.

People hunt frogs in different ways. Some just go out and grab them. Others use a gig pole, and those of us most frightened by the thought of being uncomfortably close to a water moccasin use a .22 rifle.

I guess you could say that the purists in this sport go grabbing. The trick to this is having a good operator on the boat's outboard motor. It's the job of the ship's pilot to run the boat right up to the frog without running into snake-infested banks or trees. A wrong move at the helm can produce terribly exciting consequences.

The night was really warm. Mosquitos were as thick as fleas on a dog. With no wind at all, every croak of the frogs rang like the bells of Notre Dame up and down the murky waters of the drainage canal. The heavy weed and grass cover made this a perfect spot for frogs, but also for snakes.

The grabber for this adventure was a local part Indian whose name will remain anonymous. Likewise, the name of the boat operator will continue in obscurity. Must protect the names of the guilty, don't you see?

During this adventurous frog hunt, the aforementioned frog grabber spotted a trophy class pair of frog legs still attached to a rather proud-looking bullfrog. With eyes transfixed by a spotlight, the order to move in was passed to the helmsman. Just as the boat was nearing the target, a rather large Mr. No-shoulders came into play. The rescinding of the previous order didn't reach the driver in time to prevent the inevitable meeting of grabber and biter.

The ensuing scene went something like this. As the boat came into contact with the limb on which the cottonmouth was reposing, the grabber made his way to the back of the boat in a rather large hurry. In fact, it was quite a few seconds before the ship's pilot realized the blur flying past was his mate from the bow of the boat. There being no further boat beyond the outboard motor, his feat of running along on top of the water was truly amazing. Still more amazing was the fact that the motor could be reversed in time to avoid the falling snake and the boat returned to a position capable of retrieving the fleeing frog grabber before, like the apostle Peter, he sank beneath the waves.

Perhaps this little synopsis of the events of that evening are sufficient to convince most of the reading public that a gig or a rifle are much more suitable instruments for collecting enough frog legs for a supper.

Several years ago, when the Methodist Church had a preacher by the name of Horton, I had the unique experience of frog hunting with another minister. A jeep, a light, a short-barrelled .410 single-shot shotgun, a .22 rifle, and two preachers hunting for frogs from 9 at night to 3 in the morning are a lethal combination.

The number of snakes we encountered that evening was enormous, for which Brother Jerry was constantly proclaiming, "Praise the Lord!" According to him, we were busting old Satan in the chops every time we blew away one of his look-a-likes. Levee marauders(muskrats) were also objects of our expert aim. A dozen or so frogs likewise made their way into our cooler before the hunt ended.

I was truly amazed at my partner. Most folks think that I get excited when I'm hunting. They should see Brother Jerry in action. That jeep could go backward or forward wide open while he fired away at snakes, muskrats, or frogs. Amazing! Just as I was about to mention the drainage canal that we were fast approaching, he looked over and said, "I ran off in that one last week!" It was such a relief to know that he had already made the mistake that we appeared to be heading for—NOT!

Going frog hunting with a wild preacher may be a long shot for you, but...

Whatever you do, don't be afraid to go with the long shots. Live life to its fullest every moment and be ready!

"Nevertheless, lest we offend them, go to the sea, cast in a hook, and take the fish that comes up first..." (Matthew 17:27a)

BACKLASH

Backlash! According to the dictionary, it's a quick, sharp recoil; a snarl in a reeled fishing line.

Other common terms used to describe this dilemma include "rat's nest," "snafu," or other rather earthy expressions used by aggravated fishermen when a backlash occurs with more than a little bit of frequency. In my profession, such terms aren't appropriate, nor can I find them in my copy of Roget's Pocket Thesaurus.

Thanks to a newspaper article, I received an invitation to go fishing. The lake we were to fish this warm afternoon was supposed to be a sure enough hot spot for lunker bass.

My host was extremely gracious. He had all the tackle I needed, which is good, because I don't own any fishing gear.

"The weather's perfect. Humidity's up. Temperatures down a bit. Wind's light. And, the isobars are really stacking in close together."

I just looked at him with that amazed look, as he said with a tinge of a smile, "Good fishing weather."

"Great. What're we waiting on?"

The boat was hitched to the truck and all the "stuff" was loaded in the boat.

Man, it takes an eighteen wheeler to haul all the equipment needed to bass fish these days. No wonder I don't have any of my own fishing equipment.

After a short drive, we slipped the boat in the lake and began casting crank baits. "The bass ought to love these spinner baits with the brightly-colored skirts."

With one expert cast, I discovered the true meaning of the

dictionary term "backlash." No longer was this a term to be defined. It was now a reality to be dealt with.

"Just take your time and pull on the jumbled line. When you find a loop, pull on it and then try to get the line to come on out of the reel." Such was the sage advice given to the rookie while the veteran continued to cast for lunker bass.

Honest to goodness, every other cast, I had a backlash. I adjusted the drag, as directed by my continually-casting partner. I mumbled under my breath, breathed out painful and pitiful sighs, and finally stretched out across the back of the boat to drink a cold bottle of apple juice.

All the while, my good ole buddy continued to cast and chatter. "Tired?"

"Nope."

"Wanna leave?"

"Nope."

"Want some advice?"

"Nope."

Such was the content of our lengthy and involved conversation. Every hot spot known to exist in this particular lake was carefully and completely checked out—to no avail. Every imaginable type of lure was brought forth from the myriad boxes and tried—to no avail.

As we were loading the boat, the Bill Dance of the day moaned out the comment, "I don't understand what happened."

He had no idea what had been going on in the back of the boat. While I was constantly trying to unleash the backlashes or unhook the hung lures, he was casting and casting and casting.

The sighs he heard, which he thought were sounds of frustration, were actually prayers. I was pleading with the Lord to keep the fish from biting as long as I was tied up in knots, and He did.

It may be a long shot for me to catch lunker bass. It may even be a long shot for me to catch anything more than a cold, but...

Whatever you do, don't be afraid to go with the long shots. Live life to its fullest every moment and be ready!

"Do not be deceived, God is not mocked; for whatever a man sows, that he will also reap."(Galatians 6:7)

GUN CONTROL

The debate over gun control continues to rage in our land. Certainly, when we read of some child accidently or otherwise shooting another with a handgun, we're tempted to conclude that handguns ought to be outlawed. This position is championed by Sarah Brady and Handgun Control, Inc. and our present President.

Admittedly, when I see some maniac shooting up a fast food restaurant with a semi-automatic weapon, I wonder if such weapons shouldn't be outlawed. Such a scene, rare as it actually is, is a powerful emotional tool to promote the gun control issue.

No doubt, we've all heard the arguments on both sides of the gun control debate. Those who want to ban some or all firearms say that there would be no shooting deaths if people didn't have guns. Sounds sensible on the surface, but if we care enough to dig a bit into the realities of our world, we may find other information which refutes this conclusion.

In the first place, if handguns or semi-automatic weapons, or sling shots are outlawed, who will be disarmed? Criminals? Not hardly. Firearms will be available at some price as long as they're being made anywhere in the world. There will be a black market where criminals can purchase them. The only ones who will be disarmed will be law-abiding citizens. Without the deterrent of our firearms, how safe will our homes and places of business be? Just ask local law enforcement officers if they can protect every home and business in any community 24 hours a day. Ask them if a totally disarmed citizenry makes any sense from a law enforcement point of view. Armed, law-abiding citizens are a deterrent to crime.

Sometimes firearms are used to kill people. Knives are also popular weapons. Chains, baseball bats, ropes, fists and feet are all employed by criminals to murder people, but no one is lobbying to have any of these other weapons of choice outlawed. The very idea of outlawing baseball bats would be ludicrous.

So what's the point? The point is simply this. Firearms are

used in many murders and some accidental deaths, but those firearms would have never killed a single person if someone hadn't pulled the trigger. The weapon, whatever type it happened to be, didn't kill the victim. The criminal or the careless user is the one at fault.

So goes the debate today. The National Rifle Association, which is constantly attacked by liberal media and gun control advocates, has taken the position that what we need is stiffer punishment of criminals. If someone commits a crime with a firearm, the penalty should be substantially greater. If someone uses a firearm to commit murder, that criminal should receive the death penalty automatically.

Though I agree with the NRA's position concerning stiff penalties for crimes committed with a firearm, I think the debate over gun control needs to be taken a step further.

When gun control proponents scream that guns are to blame and ought to be outlawed, they're saying that responsibility for crime lies outside the criminal. It's the guns' fault. A decade or two ago, these same people were saying that it was society's fault, the criminal's environment, his family background, the people he was running with, or the materialistic, capitalistic nation we live in.

I'm beginning to wonder when we're going to wake up and realize that criminals are responsible for their actions. Outlawing the ownership of a handgun, a semi-automatic rifle, a pump shotgun, or a compound bow will not deter crime as long as we continue to blame everything and everyone except the ones who are actually responsible, the criminals.

We are all responsible people, created in the image of God. Because of our fallen, sinful natures, however, anything is possible. It is the opinion of this writer that any ridiculous conclusion is possible when God and the responsibility of the individual are left out. Any foolish and unworkable solution is likely when people do not accept responsibility for their actions.

The actions of the criminal element in our society must be curbed. The nation which refuses to administer just punishment can expect God to inflict that punishment on society as a whole through additional crimes committed by people who should either be in jail or dead.

It's past time for us to wake up to the real issues in the gun control debate. Place the blame for violent crime where it belongs, on the criminal, not the weapon.

Bringing some sanity to the gun control debate may be a long shot, but...

Whatever you do, don't be afraid to go with the long shots. Live life to its fullest every moment and be ready!

"The Lord will strike you with the boils of Egypt, with tumors, with the scab, and with the itch, from which you cannot be healed."(Deuteronomy 28:27)

ITCHY IVY

The summer between my eighth and ninth grades didn't look very promising. I would turn fourteen half way through, and there wasn't anything special on my calendar.

The year before, I'd been inducted into the Royal Order of the Obnoxious and Rebellious Teenagers. The year following that boring summer of my fourteenth birthday, I would earn the right of passage into the driver's seat of the family car with a valid motor vehicle operator's license. I would also begin learning to play a gentleman's game, golf, but that summer of turning fourteen held nothing of promise.

I don't think my mother realized how empty my life seemed to be that summer; nevertheless, she brought the wisdom of the ages to bear on my predicament. Her solution to the doldrums of my fourteenth summer was biology.

"Why wait till your sophomore year to take biology?" she asked with an air of concern for my inactivity and consequent boredom. "Go on and take it this summer and get it out of the way."

My reaction? "Great idea, Mom! How did you ever think of such a neat thing for me to do with all my spare time during summer vacation? You're the sharpest mom on earth. I'm so grateful you thought of this." Was this really my reaction? NOT!

I pleaded my case, ignorance, which played right into her

73

hands. I gave the most reasonable argument against summer school ever presented. The logic was awesome, the emotion intense, every word dripping with sincerity. As a result of my eloquence and elocution, I was sitting in biology class the very next Monday morning.

Part of the joy of taking biology in the summer time is the abundance of bugs and plants for the proverbial collections. The flora and fauna were truly luxurious that year.

Field trips were eagerly anticipated, because they meant we could get out of the classroom for a while. We managed to overlook the muggy heat of a Mississippi summer as we traipsed through the woods in search of plants and insects for our assigned assemblages. Actually, we didn't mind the heat or the humidity, because without air conditioned classrooms, the heat was more oppressive inside than out. Our 1964 biology class is where the term "heat index" originated!

Because every member of that summer's biology class, except me, was allergic to poison ivy, I was designated the poisonous plant purloiner.

In those days, I could wallow in poison ivy and never be bothered by it. I had no idea how sneaky this three-leafed plant would prove to be. Somewhere along the line, perhaps because of over exposure to it that summer, I became as allergic to poison ivy as a hay fever sufferer to the yellow flower in the height of the goldenrod bloom.

With no prior warning, an itch sneaked up on me. I scratched the spot and received a titillating sensation, so I scratched like a dog after an illusive flea. Before I knew it, I had red whelps all over me, and the pleasurable experience of the first scratching was gone.

These days, all I have to do is walk by poison ivy and I break out. Even in the dead of winter, I contract the itchy, itchy body (akin to the achy, breaky heart, I think) from leaning against a tree with a poison ivy vine entwined about it.

If you too suffer from the itchy ivy allergy, I know exactly how you feel. If you're feeling a familiar itching sensation even now, I sense it too. You know you're seriously allergic to poison ivy when you start scratching an imaginary spot just reading about it!

Truth is, I've been "itching" to share this story with you for some time now, but the editors kept "scratching" this chapter from the manuscript!

Avoiding a bout with poison ivy this summer may be a long shot for you and me, but...

Whatever you do, don't be afraid to go with the long shots. Live life to its fullest every moment and be ready!

"Remember His marvelous works which He has done, His wonders and the judgments of His mouth."(1 Chronicles 16:12)

MEMORIES

Memories—can be pleasant or painful. Some of my memories of earlier days are filled with laughter and happiness, of good times with family and friends. Other memories are rather painful. Memories of an alcoholic father threatening our lives with a butcher knife is an example of the latter. Thankfully, those memories are smothered by the memory of a father, gone since 1976, who died sober as a recovered and recovering alcoholic.

All of us want to hold on to the good memories, but sometimes it's so hard. Memories too often fade with the passage of time.

How can we keep our pleasant memories alive? One thing we can do to keep memories alive is to realize that memories aren't just to be enjoyed. Good memories ought to be passed along to the next generation by giving the younger ones similar opportunities to build their own memories.

My brother is twelve years my senior and had many early experiences with relatives whom I never got to know. He spent many happy times on the Gulf Coast fishing and fooling around with our grandparents before they moved to Jackson.

One evening, we were eating out with our mother and her sister from Oregon, and the conversation turned to the old days, fishing from the piers and crabbing along the coast and so forth. Sonny, my brother(real name, Thomas), said, "You know, those memories are so sweet. I can still smell the salt air, hear the tide crashing on the beach, and see the seagulls floating by, looking for a hand-out from the fishermen."

Then he said something that touched my heart and soul and set me to thinking about this chapter. He said something that needs to be repeated. Memories are so much sweeter when you take the time to give another generation their own set of memories.

For my brother, the opportunity to pay back the debt of a million memories given him by family comes in the form of a precious grandson. Bryant Thomas is a bright, loving child, the only male grandchild in the family.

Whenever the opportunity presents itself, "Pop" takes Bryant Thomas out fishing or just playing in the backyard under the pine trees. My brother's namesake will never forget the wind in his face as he and his Pop race across Barnett Reservoir in "Pop's boat." The memories of the wading pool under the trees that hold cooing doves, raucous blue jays, and cheerful red birds will always be vivid. The greatest memory of all, however, will be of a grandfather who loves him and would literally give his life, if need be, for him.

Perhaps there are some children in your life, grandchildren or just next door neighbors. When you start thinking about your memories, why not go out and help create some new ones for those little fellows? It will be one of the greatest gifts they'll ever receive.

Creating memories for someone else may be a long shot for you, but...

Whatever you do, don't be afraid to go with the long shots. Live life to its fullest every moment and be ready!

"In them He has set a tabernacle for the sun...It's rising is from one end of heaven, and its circuit to the other end; and there is nothing hidden from its heat."(Psalms 19:4c,6)

IN THE HEAT OF THE HUNT

Ernest Cobb and I rode out to the our deer camp the other Saturday for a look see and discovered once again that hunting is hard work. The dogs had to be fed, watered, and sprayed for ticks and fleas. The grass needed a few rounds with the "Poppin" John Deere tractor, and the soybean and corn crops needed a check for signs of animal predation.

To tell the truth, I don't know how a hound dog survives in the heat of a Mississippi August. After watching them pant and shuffle about trying to find a cool, shady spot on the concrete slab, I understand why they call these "the dog days of summer." It's hotter than a japeleno pepper at a Mexican fiesta.

Since the grass was already neck deep around the camp house, I thought it might be a good idea for me to take the tractor and make a few rounds to knock the weeds down a bit. After about an hour, the tractor suddenly died. Ernest looked over at me as if to say, "Why'd ya quit?"

Not needing an interpreter, I answered, "I guess it just ran hot!"

Ernest's verbal response? "One of ya did, that's for sure."

Having tended to the dogs and the grass, we turned our

attention to the crops and the aforementioned animal predation. The beans and corn were both pretty; the beans waist deep, and the corn head high to a horse.

A check of the soybeans revealed a high interest in them from the deer herd. The beans around the edges were already stripped to the main stalk. Trails as wide as ole Jethro's foot (Beverly Hillbillies, that is) lead into and sometimes all the way through the field. In the mind of this deer hunter, that hillside of soybeans was fast becoming my "Field of Dreams."

The corn also revealed some serious attention from the local chapter of the Royal Order of the Raccoon. The neighborhood bandits knew every single corn cob in the four-acre patch and the exact hour when it would be perfectly mature.

A quick check with our friend and neighbor, Milton, who lives down the road, revealed how serious the corn 'n coon situation had become. We asked Milton if he'd ease down there at night and try to thin out the number of thieves making off with the corn. Milton assured us that he had been making every effort to do just that, but "Them ain't your normal, everyday, run-of-the-mill coons. They's educated coons."

"Say what?" we both chimed in simultaneously in response to the latter part of his description of the situation in the corn patch.

Milton said, "When I ease up to the corn, I can hear the little beggars working, but when I turn on my spotlight, they's just too smart. They cover up they eyes with their hands(and he demonstrated just how the coons do it) and wait for me to turn out the light. They know the light'll reflect off they eyes and git 'em kilt."

We all had a good laugh with Milton's explanation for his inability to control the coon predation in the corn patch, but urged him to keep trying. Maybe he can take the beagle hound that wears the grocery store bag and let him slip up on the coons while they've got their hands over their eyes! Maybe he can catch them in the sack and roll his one eye in an attempt to say, "It's in the bag!"

Sweltering through the August heat, waiting as patiently as possible for cooler weather and the opening of deer season in October might be a long shot for you like it is for me, but...

Whatever you do, don't be afraid to go with the long shots.
Live life to its fullest every moment and be ready!

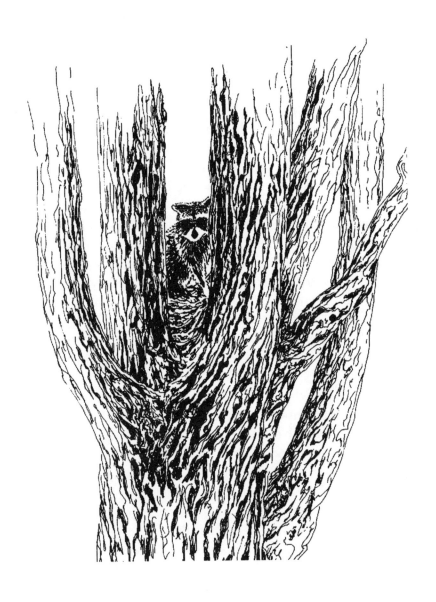

"Now the serpent was more cunning than any beast of the field which the Lord God had made."(Genesis 3:1)

SNAKES!

Most normal human beings have a healthy aversion to snakes. A small percentage of us are down right terrified of any and every slithering serpent we see. Then there is that minuscule percentage of the non-institutionalized population who love snakes, have them as pets, and even play with them, for heaven's sake!

I used to say that there were only two kinds of snakes, dead and ought-to-be dead, but a hunting buddy from another small town gave a new twist to that old saying. "There are only two kinds of snakes—rattlesnakes and moccasins, both of which are dangerous and should be killed on sight!"

Before you snake-aholics out there throw a fit and get your scales all out of balance, let me hasten to add that I have mellowed somewhat in my old age.

On occasion, I have let a snake live. The circumstances have to be just right for me to weaken to that point, however. I have to be totally unarmed and caught completely off guard. In addition, I must be stepping into the pulpit at 11:00 on Sunday morning. You see, at that point, I have a much larger serpent that I plan to bludgeon with the Word.

Even those of us who are terribly frightened by snakes love a good snake story. And I have a good one for you. You thought so, didn't you?

George Cunningham, first cousin to one of my infamous flock, Wick Eatherly, is one of those human beings on the fringe of sanity. George loves snakes and fears them not!

George and I were riding three-wheelers one sunny afternoon when we came upon a cottonmouth moccasin thoroughly enjoying himself in the midst of a mudpuddle. As if on cue, the snake reared up and flung open its wide white mouth as George stopped at the edge of the murky water. With no regard for life or limb, George reached out and patted the snake on the head like it was his favorite lab. Well, the stroke was a might quicker than it would have been if it had been man's best friend.

The snake dutifully slithered back down into the water, then quickly reappeared in the same threatening posture. This time George held one hand in front of the snake to occupy his attention while he reached and caught the snake behind the head with his other hand.

Even though I was impatiently revving up my ATV motor a quarter of a mile away, I could see the devilment in George's eyes. Knowing how petrified I am of snakes, it was obvious to me that he was planning to come after me with that dang serpent.

Well folks, the starting gun had been fired, the gate swung open, and the race was on. The Honda was screaming for me to back off the rpm's, but George was gaining on me. Trees were whizzing by so fast the bark was being sucked off by the backdraft. Neither sawbriars nor muscadine vines were an impediment to me and the thundering three-wheeler.

Then catastrophe struck. My glance back to check on George's progress resulted in a quick decision to disembark from the machine to avoid a very large tree. Three-wheeler went left. Preacher went right.(always the conservative, don't you see?)

After a couple of bumps, flops, and rolls, I was on my feet running for all I was worth. Like in the cartoons, my legs were pumping, my feet churning up the soft earth, but I wasn't getting anywhere. I was running in place, and the place was quickly becoming unsuitable for human habitation!

Just as George and the snake arrived, my tennis shoe grippers caught. Mud flew. Blinded by muddy missiles, George temporarily terminated his pursuit. But after a couple of seconds, he was once again speeding after me, maniacal grin, fiendish laugh and all.

An old, abandoned tenant house was within range. The

distance to the front door was covered in world-record time. The old weathered cypress door nearly came off its hinges as it swung open and shut in one smooth move.

As I stood just inside the door, panting like a deer that had been chased all morning by a pack of hungry walker dogs, I failed to notice a gap of some six to eight inches between the bottom of the door and the plank floor.

George snickered as he stepped up on the porch. Though he gave the door a good shove, there was no way he was going to open it!

Then it happened. Before I had a chance to react, he noticed the gap under the door. He caught hold of my leg and pulled so hard that I fell down kicking and screaming. I don't think anyone ever pulled my leg quite that hard before.

How hard did he pull my leg? About as hard as I've been pulling yours with this whole story!

Whether your snake stories are honest-to-goodness true or slightly exaggerated like mine, I truly hope that close encounters with snakes will be a long shot for you, but...

Whatever you do, don't be afraid to go with the long shots. Live life to its fullest every moment and be ready!

"Then God said, 'Let there be lights in the firmament of the heavens to divide the day from the night; and let them be for signs and seasons, and for days and years; and let them be for lights in the firmament of the heavens to give light on the earth,' and it was so. Then God made two great lights; the greater light to rule the day, and the lesser light to rule the night. He made the stars also. God set them in the firmament of the heavens to give light on the earth, and to rule over the day and over the night, and to divide the light from the darkness. And God saw that it was good. So the evening and the morning were the fourth day." (Genesis 1:14-19)

LAYING OUT

Every now and then, one of my harem of hens will pop up and announce, "I'm gonna lay out, okay Dad?" I don't understand why people with seemingly sound minds want to lay out and cook themselves. As long as I don't have to join in, I don't mind so much. But once in a great while, the four females gang up on me, put on their most pitiful expressions and plead, "Please take us to the beach this summer."

84

Our culture worships tanned hides for some reason. My idea of a tanned hide is a mounted ten-point buck! Bronze humans are supposed to be more beautiful. Sun-tanned skin is supposed to be sensual and seductive.

Well, as a red-headed, fair-skinned male, I've never been able to tan. All my best efforts end in that well-done look. Red might look good on some folks, but the sun leaves me looking red as a beet, and that ain't so pretty.

I remember a trip to the Gulf Coast when I was a kid. We were there for a few days of fun in the sun and sand. I spent three hours romping up and down the beach the first afternoon we were there. The next morning, I was in incredible pain, so red I looked like a piece of raw meat. It took days and days of Solarcaine and much, much suffering to get over the wonderful experience of fun on the beach.

From that day forward, I've avoided the beach like the plague. In my mind, sand plus sun equals pain, which is something I don't enjoy in the least.

For those who can't find any sun during the winter or on cloudy days, tanning booths are now available even in the Mississippi Delta. It amazes me that sensible people will pay for pain with their hard-earned dollars.

The medical profession is constantly warning us about the harmful effects of too much sun. All that laying out is going to give folks serious skin problems. I've known that since I was a kid.

Thankfully, my wife and children all have sensitive skin. They've already discovered that laying out is painful. The only thing that saves me from a fate worse than death(a vacation on the beach) is their realizing that they're also going to get burned. Oh, glorious pain. It does have its good side after all.

On a recent excursion to the golf course, someone called attention to my rather pale-looking legs. I don't know why I had on shorts, but I did. It's terrible how some folks make fun of my WHITE legs.

"I'll have you know," I retorted in mock indignation, "that I've spent about a week a month, laying out all night under a full moon, working on this lunar tan."

A cool night with no mosquitoes, sitting in a swing with my lovely wife is my idea of "laying out". I won't get a tan, but the hugs, kisses, and twinkling eyes make it a far, far better thing I do.

Getting a tan by moonlight may be a long shot, but . . .

Whatever you do, don't be afraid to go with the long shots. Live life to its fullest every moment and be ready!

"How shall we escape if we neglect so great a salvation, which at first began to be spoken by the Lord, and was confirmed to us by those who heard Him, God also bearing witness both with signs and wonders, with various miracles, and gifts of the Holy Spirit, according to His own will?" (Hebrews 2:3-4)

MIRACLES

Theologians who claim to know more about the Bible than some of us simple folks say that miracles have ceased, that God no longer performs supernatural wonders. They say that there's no more parting of the waters or walking on them; no more raising the dead; no more feeding 5,000 people with a couple of small fish and a few loaves of bread.

Well, I don't know about you, but I beg to differ with those who say that miracles don't happen today. In fact, some of these folks say that miracles never did happen, that the folks who wrote the Bible just had vivid imaginations.

A seminary(school for preachers) that I won't name, but one I considered going to(and am now glad I didn't!), had a professor who explained away as many of Jesus' miracles as he could. He told his students that Jesus never fed 5,000 people with a couple of fish and a few loaves of bread. "That's ridiculous," the skeptical prof intoned to his class. Jesus asked that little boy to share his food and then set him before the crowd as a good example. The people just followed the little boy's example, and that's how Jesus fed the 5,000. Hogwash!

I do believe in miracles, but because this is supposed to be outdoor humor, let me move on quickly to share some mighty miraculous events from the natural world. I've seen doves flying off with their hearts shot clean out. I've seen full-grown turkey gobblers no more than twenty steps from me in the wide open simply disappear into thin air. I've even seen deer shot dead as a hammer, suddenly jump up and run off, never to be seen again. Humor me, now, as I relate just a couple of these miraculous events.

It was on a turkey hunt in central New Mexico (my first turkey hunt ever outside of Mississippi), that I briskly strolled, then slowly walked, staggered a bit, and finally crawled up the rock strewn mountain trail to a ridge between two imposing peaks. When I could finally hear again above my wheezing lungs and pounding heart, I tried calling a turkey. The response was immediate—but way off down the OTHER side of the mountain.

"Tough luck, ole boy," but this imitation she-turkey just ain't coming. After the climb to the ridge, I was determined that the rest of the day's hunt was going to be downhill all the way.

After a couple of minutes, I tried calling again. I figured I'd try one more time before starting my descent back toward camp. Well sir, the ole boy gobbled up what I had teasingly tossed his way. He was already up on the ridge with me.

Knowing how narrow the ridge was and that there was no way he could get around behind me like so many turkey gobblers have done before, I got positioned and had the shotgun ready. I was breathing rapidly again, waiting, waiting, waiting. About the time I thought something was wrong, the turkey gobbled—right behind me! I mean, the guy wasn't any more than twenty steps from me. I cut my eyes around at him, and then the miracle happened. Realizing that this situation wasn't right, he disappeared. The next thing I knew, he was 75 yards from me, and heading off back down the mountain from whence he came. Don't tell me miracles don't happen!

Then there was the miracle that happened to the now infamous James "Hoggie" Hargraves. Aiming carefully with his prized new .50 caliber muzzleloader, he squeezed the trigger. Baloooom! When the smoke cleared, there lay the huge doe.

Proud as peaches, Hoggie rested the rifle on his lap, took out a cigarette, and lit up. He was sitting there chuckling to himself about how easy muzzleloader hunting was when he noticed that one of the doe's back legs moved—ever so slightly. It was so faint a twitch he wasn't sure that he actually saw it.

When it moved again, Hoggie pitched the cigarette and began scuffling to reload his rifle. Unless a pack of wild Indians are attacking, it usually takes a good minute or more to reload one of these primitive weapons. While the frenzied effort to reload went on, all four legs began to move. As Hoggie stood with mouth agape and gun still unloaded, the dead deer got to her feet and ran, not trotted, not walked; I mean RAN off.

Hoggie was so overcome by the miracle and so frustrated by the unfolding scene that he tracked the deer across a public road and got lost! He couldn't find his way back to his stand. Every time he came back to that gravel road, which he couldn't remember crossing, he'd turn and go back in the wrong direction. Miracles can do amazing things to us, can't they Hog?

I would sure like to continue telling you about doves, ducks, and quail that have repeated the miracle of flying through a hail of lead and steel without so much as a scratch, but I guess I better stop for now.

You may never have witnessed an honest-to-goodness miracle. You may even think that ever seeing a miracle, much less experiencing one, is a real long shot, but...

Whatever you do, don't be afraid to go with the long shots. Live life to its fullest every moment and be ready!

"Therefore you shall make images of your tumors and images of your rats that ravage the land, and you shall give glory to the God of Israel; perhaps He will lighten His hand from you, from your gods, and from your land." (I Samuel 6:5)

CRITTERS

I'm constantly amazed at the things we're afraid of. Some of us are afraid of mice. Others of spiders, roaches, frogs, crickets, or other various and sundry creepy crawlers. Critters, most everybody is afraid of one kind or another.

Around our house, at least one of us is afraid of everything that crawls. The peaceful bliss of a quiet evening is subject to annihilation by frightened females at any time. It's like living on a Strategic Air Command base. You never know when the alarm will be sounded and it's time to scramble.

Once upon a time, I was relaxing, allowing the hectic hubub of the day's activities to ooze away. At the precise moment that my heart rate, breathing, and blood pressure all reached appropriate levels for continued good health, a blood-curdling scream reverberated through the walls as though they weren't there at all.

It's amazing how a middle-aged man can go from the easy chair, semi-prone position, through the rotation necessary to become upright, and halfway down the hall in one move. If I hadn't done it, I wouldn't have believed it myself. A scream of such sheer terror can cause one to do wondrous things.

What prompted this discharge of dread? Dorothy was visiting the little girl's room when a tiny mouse peeped out at her from under the bathmat, which was only a foot or so from her feet. I honestly don't understand what went on in the narrow confines of that bathroom.

Minnie Mouse didn't mean a thing by her appearance, but much to her surprise and Dorothy's, the reaction to her presence was startling, to say the least. Dorothy screamed! Minnie raced swiftly for the door. This latter move blocked said female's only avenue of escape, which, of course, brought forth another round of raw terror.

I raced for the bedroom(which I had to go through to get to the bathroom), knowing that Dorothy or one of the girls was injured terribly. Wham!(Why does the woman always lock the bedroom door when she has to go see Mr. Donovan?)

A bobby pin was quickly retrieved from the other bathroom, and the lock was soon disengaged. I sure wish it had been that easy to get my face removed from the door!

Once inside the bedroom, I called out, "What's wrong? Are you hurt? What is it? Where are you? What's happened?"

"If you'd quit asking so many questions, I'd answer some of them."

"Okay, what happened?"

"Thank you. There's a mouse in here."

"All that commotion over a little ole mouse?"

"Yes."

"Where is it now?"

"Out there somewhere!"

"Okay, I'll get the broom and waylay the little sucker." When I returned, Dorothy was still in the throne room, having ascended to the highest point available.

"Why are you still in there?"

"The mouse ran back in here before I could get out."

The bobby pin was employed once again. One thing's for sure, when we got married in 1974, it wasn't nearly as difficult to carry her across the threshold as it was to get her out of that bathroom! Actually, this happened some years back when Dorothy was thoroughly expecting our third urchin.

Actually, I only made it as far as the door leading out of the bathroom into the bedroom. Once I set her down, she bounded nearly ten feet from the door of the bathroom to the bed. It was an awesome gravity-defying flight. If she had managed a marquee of flashing lights, I would have sworn that the Goodyear blimp was passing through our bedroom! No doubt the sign would have read, "BUY DE-CON MOUSE KILLER!"

While Dorothy employed the bed as a trampoline, I returned to my dastardly duty. Just as I expected, the mouse was once again under the bathmat.

Throwing it aside with one hand, I sought to squish the racing rodent with the broom. In case you've never tried it, wielding a broom with one hand while in a squatting position and dodging a mouse at the same time isn't all that easy.

The poor, terrified creature ran between my legs, at which juncture I repeated my earlier feat of levitation.

I hollered. Dorothy squealed with glee at my apparent dread of the tiny creature. I swiveled in mid-air and made one desperate but successful stroke with the broom. Remember, I'm good at one-hand wonders.

The mouse was struck, in the midst of a mad dash across the carpet. It's truly amazing how high a mouse on carpet bounces when struck with a flimsy straw object. The mortified mouse flew through the air with the greatest of ease and landed right on the bed.

Needless to say, guess who had the last laugh? Doctors tell us that laughter is good medicine. It's true! I've been in good health ever since.

Maybe you're afraid of mice, too. Or is it roaches, spiders, frogs, or perhaps the dark? Dealing with your trepidations may be a long shot, but...

Whatever you do, don't be afraid to go with the long shots. Live life to its fullest every moment and be ready!

"Listen, for I will speak of excellent things, and from the opening of my lips will come right things; for my mouth will speak truth; wickedness is an abomination to my lips. All the words of my mouth are with righteousness; nothing crooked or perverse is in them. They are all plain to him who understands, and right to those who find knowledge." (Proverbs 8:6-9)

TRUTH, NOTHING BUT THE TRUTH

What with Bambi, Donald Duck, Bugs Bunny, and of course, Yogi Bear, it's no small wonder that we hunters can still legally pursue our love of the chase. Thanks to animal rights extremists, hunters have been given a bum wrap, a black eye, and a bad name.

Contrary to the opinion of some, however, hunters are not murderers of poor, innocent creatures. Hunters, for the most part, are the reason we have large numbers of such critters as deer, turkeys, and ducks, not to mention non-game species as well.

Realizing that the true facts about hunters and hunting won't change the minds of those who don't want to be confused by truth, I want to appeal to the rest of the reading population. The vast majority of those who care enough about our environment to read up on the subject, I believe, are intelligent, sensible people. In other words, I'm appealing to you, the reader, to listen for a few moments.

Ever heard of Pittman-Robertson? Don't feel too bad if you haven't. Properly identified as the Federal Aid in Wildlife Restoration Act of 1937, this is one of the few federal programs that has honestly worked, and worked well.

This legislation placed a ten-percent federal excise tax on rifles, shotguns, archery equipment, handguns, and ammunition. The U.S. Fish and Wildlife Service(FWS) uses eight-percent of the funds for administrative purposes, the remainder going to state wildlife agencies.

Another great achievement of hunters has come through the duck stamp program. To help pay for federal programs such as wildlife and waterfowl refuges, Congress instituted the duck stamp program. Hunters through the years have supported conservation efforts with over $7 billion through license fees, $4.5 billion through federally generated funds, and a half billion dollars in duck stamp revenues.

Wild-eyed, mis-informed, opinionated, liberal(that about does it for now) environmentalists make lots of noise and pass out tons of propaganda which national media regurgitate with impunity. They claim to be concerned with saving the poor creatures of the forest from us blood-thirsty, bullet-crazed hunters.

Well, the facts say otherwise. State wildlife agencies derive 58% of their funds directly from hunting and fishing license sales and interest on those funds, another 25% from federal aid(Pittman/Robertson monies), and only 17% from general appropriations. Since 80% of the people in the southeast engage in outdoor activities, we can safely say that a lion's share of those latter funds also come from hunters and fishermen.

If animal rights groups genuinely cared, they would stop all the loud talk and start trying to match out of their own pockets what hunters have done out of concern for wildlife. Twelve billion dollars, to date, is nothing to sneeze at.

A recent article by one of the more vocal anti-hunting groups, for example, claimed that hunters don't care about nongame species. Well, when state agencies proposed checkoffs on tax returns, nongame stamps, bond issues, art contests, resident taxes, and even begging, the funds that came in were paltry indeed.

When Congress proposed a bill in the 1970's to tax such items as bird seed, birdhouses, and other items used to enjoy and enhance nongame species, the cries could be heard from Washington D.C. to Washington State!

Colorado tried the very same approach as Pittman/Robertson for nongame wildlife conservation and restoration in 1974. It failed. Why? Lack of funds. Guess who purchased 63% of the nongame stamps that were bought? You guessed it. Hunters and fishermen. Now I ask you, "Where were the hypocrites who were crying about the lack of concern for nongame species?" The majority of those who were concerned enough to contribute were blood-thirsty hunters!

Hunters, to their detriment, haven't talked much about what they've done to preserve our wildlife resources. Some would say that it's tooting our own horn. There are times when tooting your own horn is the only way it gets tooted. While the extremists have harangued in front of T.V. cameras and illegally harassed law-abiding hunters, hunters have been quietly doing many good things to save our wildlife resources($12 billion).

When it comes to killing poor Bambi or Donald Duck, I guess I'm guilty. I'm guilty of shooting a deer rather than sitting at home in front of the idiot box and allowing the deer to starve to death because of over-crowding. I would rather eat venison than let it rot. When it comes to Donald Duck, I have a problem. When we hunted with lead shot, most ducks I shot and hit, fell and were faithfully retrieved by my lab, Kelly. With this sorry, no account steel shot, many more birds lose a pillow-full of feathers and fly off to die somewhere out of sight. The meat is lost, but the environmentalists have saved two bald eagles in the process.

Thousands of lost ducks versus a couple of questionable eagle deaths is not the kind of sensible game management we need. But it's what we get when we allow animal rights groups to dictate policy.

Sounds terrible, doesn't it? Well, there is yet hope. I've discovered a way to get a limit of ducks without using steel shot. When the ducks hear me calling, they rain down out of the sky like stove wood, roll over on their backs and drown themselves in tears of laughter!

Hunting may not be your cup of tea, but I hope you now have a better understanding of hunting and its place in the preservation and management of our wildlife resources.

Taking a nice buck with a bow or rifle may be a long shot for you. Downing a duck with nothing but a call may be an even longer shot, but...

Whatever you do, don't be afraid to go with the long shots. Live life to its fullest every moment and be ready!

"And there is no creature hid from His sight, but all things are naked and open to the eyes of Him to whom we must give account." (Hebrews 4:13)

HAMPTON COURT PALACE

After I'd served nearly ten years as pastor of the Presbyterian Church in Belzoni, the congregation and community got together and sent Dorothy and me on a trip to Merry Old England. One of the highlights of that trip was a visit to Hampton Court Palace, which was built by Cardinal Wolsey for King Henry VIII. In reality, I think the church leader was afraid of losing his head if he didn't do something dramatic, and this enormous palace and its adjacent palatial gardens definitely qualified for dramatic.

Here in Belzoni, we have some descendants of the Hampton's, for whom the palace was named. One in particular is a member of our congregation whose story is as worthy of note as the sprawling splendor of Hampton Court is of a visit if you're ever in England.

Sam Hampton came into this world just after the turn of the century. Teddy was President and was speaking softly and carrying a big ole stick when he came to the Mississippi Delta to hunt bear. One can still buy Teddy Bears at Onward store on Highway 61 north of Vicksburg. The landscape has changed a great deal since the days of Teddy and the birth of Sam Hampton.

At the turn of the Twentieth Century, the Mississippi Delta was one huge swamp. Except for a few plantations along the Mississippi, Yazoo and Sunflower Rivers, huge stands of virgin timber and canebrake thickets commanded the landscape. Snakes and mosquitos kept most would-be settlers at bay.

A few adventurous souls braved the elements, gambled against the odds, and came down out of the hills to take on the wilderness we now call home. One of those early families was a clan named Hampton.

Born on December 10, 1907, Belzoni resident Sam Hampton shares stories about what the Mississippi flatlands looked like in the early days of the twentieth century. The Delta was a wild, untamed land teeming with critters, some of which we no longer see prowling about.

The eastern end of Humphreys County, known as Mathena, was home to the Hampton's in those days. Growing up in the big woods before all the timber was cut and the land cleared for farming planted the seeds of hunting, fishing, and trapping deep in young Sam. His forefathers were cut of the same mold. He remembers looking up to his great-grandfather as a role model, which makes sense, cause the gentleman was 7 feet tall and weighed nearly 400 pounds!

About the time Uncle Sam called for America's young men to go "over there" in 1917, little Sam Hampton was becoming a real woodsman. He tells of watching black bears wading through the ditches and bayous, catching turtles and throwing them against huge white oak tree trunks to bust the shells so they could feast on soft-shell turtle.

The nighttime stillness in those days was often broken by howling wolves as they travelled in packs, chasing deer. Decaying carcasses and bleached bones testified of the speed and tenacity of these long-gone predators.

Bobcats were everywhere, as were their cousins, the panthers. Just thinking about the blood-curdling cry of a panther in the deep woods made the hair stand up on the back of the storyteller's head, like static electricity, as he related the tale of the visitor who dropped by for a spell during the Great War.

The man was the best .22 rifle shot the youngster had ever seen. If he took ten .22 short rifle cartridges to the woods, he brought back at least ten squirrels. One evening, the expert marksman roosted a wild turkey. Next morning he went back and bagged his bird. With his prize slung over his shoulder, he started out of the swamp. Suddenly something knocked him to the ground, and before he could regain his feet and composure, the trophy bird was gone in a cloud of feathers and a shower of leaves. The panther left several deep scratches on the man's neck and shoulder as well as an education about paying attention in the woods.

Listening to the stories of deer, turkey, squirrels, rabbits, quail, ducks, wolves, bobcats, panthers, and 12-foot rattlesnakes with 32 rattlers captivated my attention for an hour or more. Except for the rattlesnakes, it made me wish for the good old days, or at least the success of CRP(the Conservation Reserve Program), which promises that part of this great land will be grown up in hardwood timber once again one of these days.

Conversation with this octogenarian also points up the importance of our older generation to the rest of us. Young people, take the time to sit down and spend some quiet hours with your grandparents and your older neighbors. They have lots to offer you. Your life will be richer for the time you spend with them.

Seeing the Delta teeming with bear, wolves, panthers, and all the other critters of old may be a long shot. Hearing about it from those who saw it that way doesn't have to be, but...

Whatever you do, don't be afraid to go with the long shots. Live life to its fullest every moment and be ready!

"And afterward I will send for many hunters . . ."
(Jeremiah 16:16b)

PIGEON ROOST ROUT

Not long ago, I received an invitation to my first ever pigeon hunt. Never had I experienced more than a slight twinge of desire to shoot this corpulent cousin of the mourning dove. But in the middle of August, with no hunting seasons open, any invitation was both welcome and exciting.

The setting was a small Delta community named Isola in which resides a pigeon population conservatively estimated at some 5,000 birds. Just imagine the pollution problems created when that many feathery fiends descend upon the trees, homes, buildings, and power lines within the boundaries of a town of 500 or so friendly people and a couple of old sore heads!

The owners of a grain storage facility and an abandoned cotton gin asked some of our local expert wing shooters to come cure some of their pigeon problems with an afternoon shoot. As you can imagine, when they asked for expert wing shooters, I was naturally one of the first to receive a call...NOT!

Actually, just about everyone who was even a half-way decent shot was too busy to help out, so in desperation and at the last minute, the organizers buzzed my phone. Having gotten wind of Operation Pigeon Roost Rout, I was filled with glee when the invitation finally came in.

"Richard?"

"Yea?"

"Whatcha gonna do this afternoon?"

"What time this afternoon?"

"About thirty minutes from now."(I told you it was a last-minute invitation.)

"Nothin'."

"Reckon you could bring Ruth(my eldest) to help out with Operation Pigeon..."

I didn't let him finish the sentence. "Ruth?! What do you mean, Ruth?"

"Well, actually, I've seen you and Ruth shoot."

"That's enough of that nonsense. You're pulling my leg, right?"

"Okay, since she's too young to drive and you'll have to bring her up, you might as well bring a shotgun and a case or two of shells. You might manage to get a few."

Ignoring insults is part of every seminary's ministerial curriculum. Preachers have to learn how to act as though they are either too dumb to have noticed an insult or too spiritual to be hurt or angered by it. Having worked on ignoring insults on numerous occasions, I thanked my host and asked Ruth if she'd like to go along.

When we arrived for the shoot, we were told to check in with the local police chief to make sure everything was cleared. The chief of police/chief investigator/traffic control officer/radio operator(told you it was a small town) rose to meet me as I entered City Hall.

"Can I help you?"

"Yea. I'm here for the pigeon shoot."

"You mean they asked you to come shoot pigeons inside the city limits? Everybody in the county knows about your incredible marksmanship with a shotgun."

With my most humble air of modesty, I replied, "Well, thank you."

"Thank you." he wailed. "I'll have to evacuate the women and children. We'll have to board up the windows. We may even have to declare a state of emergency."

I love it when people put on mock demonstrations of fear and panic, don't you?

After calling a local physician and obtaining a tranquilizer for the crazed chief, we went out to the old cotton gin. Ruth took a likely spot near one corner of the gin and promptly began to drop

100

pigeons as they floated past. I honestly don't understand why they fly by her in slow motion, practically committing suicide in front of her, but when they get to me, they're somewhere near mach 2, executing all types of dipping and diving evasive actions.

Naturally, Ruth hits...I miss. The whole scene was getting out of hand until I discovered a hide-out the pigeons were using. The old cotton seed house was chock full of pigeons, and I discovered that by pitching rocks at one end, the pigeons would exit the other end one at a time. Before my throwing arm ran completely out of steam, I managed to garner a respectable number of critters as my part of the offering for the day.

Actually, we did have a pigeon hunt, and it was somewhat successful. Ruth really did take more birds than I, but I was shooting a .410 single shot and left early. Two excuses are better than none!

Believing the Pigeon Roost Rout story may be a long shot, but...

Whatever you do, don't be afraid to go with the long shots. Live life to its fullest every moment and be ready!

"Let their eyes be darkened, so that they do not see; and make their loins shake continually."(Psalms 69:23)

COONS

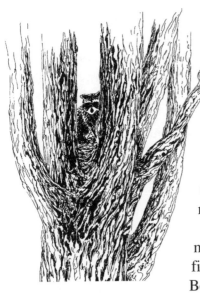

Opening weekend of squirrel and either-sex bow and arrow deer seasons came and went like the burning off of early morning fog. Reports coming in from hunters in the area indicated fair success with deer hunting and tremendous success with squirrels.

As usual, whenever there's more than one season open, I can't figure out which critters to hunt.

Before ole Sol appeared one crisp Saturday morning, I was already headed for my favorite persimmon tree and the conviction that there would be fresh tenderloin in the Wiman fridge come Saturday night.

As I eased into the edge of the woods, I heard a noise and paused. The beam from my 5-cell Mag flashlight illuminated Mr. Armadillo. I tipped on toward my tree stand.

When the light was good enough to see around my stand, the squirrel family showed up. The top of a huge water oak shook like San Francisco did back in 1989! Hulls and a few stray acorns rained down, and speaking of rain, before it was over, for the third Saturday in a row, I got soaked by another shower!

For nearly four hours, my interest was kept up though by the scurrying of the high rise rodents of Holmes County. I sat there thinking, "I knew I shoulda squirrel hunted this morning." Rifle and shotgun reports came from all points of the compass as local squirrel hunters filled their limit of eight. Some hunters I know used a whole lot more ammunition than should have been necessary and only brought in two squirrels. What about it, Ernest?

Having resolved to do a bit of squirrel hunting in the afternoon in order to honor a commitment to bring some of the limb rats home to recuperating church member, David James, I returned to the area of my deer stand around 3:00. A cat squirrel observed my entrance and began to bark his distress. Because he couldn't shut his mouth(something that gets a whole lot of us in trouble), a perfect shot brought him to my game bag.

After a short while, the performance was repeated by yet another grey squirrel. The results? The same, of course. A perfect shot didn't ruin any meat. The running gear(back legs) and drive shaft(tenderloin) from those two tender young squirrels would make some mighty fine squirrel and dumplings, fried squirrel and gravy, or stew. Either way, I sure hoped to get invited to taste test the fruit of the hunt, which, as it turned out, I didn't!

Completing my promise, I put the squirrels and rifle up, got my bow, and climbed back into the stand. Around 5:00, two nice raccoons approached, feeding on acorns and searching for some of the sweet persimmons that were still falling.

Since the premier coon cooker of the county is a member of our congregation, I decided to try and arrow one for the pot. I waited until they were really close, then drew back the bow. The arrow jumped off the rest! I eased it back, but by then, was so shook up that I missed.

Coon #1 departed posthaste while coon #2 stood and watched. I nocked a second arrow, drew back, and watched with much chagrin as it too jumped off the rest. I reckon I was shaking so much by that time that no arrow had enough balance to stay put. As I tried to ease the arrow back on the rest, I dropped it. Clang, bam, flop, and plop; down to the ground it clattered, and you can imagine what happened to coon #2. Exit stage right!

"Gee," I mused in the after-action mental examination, "If that had been a deer, just what would I have done?" By now you're probably wondering why on earth I bow hunt. Well, it's really good for my cardiovascular system. By the time I get all worked up and excited, my heart is pumping so hard that no self-respecting cholesterol could cling to the walls of my arteries even if it wanted to. You see, bow hunting is good for my health. At least, that's what I tell my lovely wife!

Hunting may not be on your agenda as part of an over-all exercise program for personal fitness. In fact, you might even say that health through hunting is a long shot, but...

Whatever you do, don't be afraid to go with the long shots. Live life to its fullest every moment and be ready!

"Then Jesus said to him, 'Unless you people see signs and wonders, you will by no means believe.' " (John 4:48)

WONDERS NEVER CEASE TO BE

Wonders never cease to be, do they? A friend emceed a major event recently, finely attired in a tux. Afterwards, I told him of the wonder I had seen.

"What's that?" he asked, taking the bait I had dangled before him.

"I saw a turkey in a monkey suit!" His face turned red, and after clearing my throat a couple of times, I exited his office.

Then there was the tennis match I observed the other evening. The wonder I beheld was incredible.

One of the participants leaped mightily into the air to return a high lob shot.

"Why's that a wonder?" you ask.

Well, though his was a tremendous leap, his tennis shoes never cleared the court. It was truly a wonder that he could leap so mightily without his shoes detaching themselves from the ground. What a wonder!

Another wonder confronted me on a turkey hunt with a friend who lives about an hour away, further south. The young man and his wife live near the small community of Tinsley, Mississippi. Truthfully, it's a wonder anyone ever finds Tinsley, but that isn't this wonder.

At about 4:45 in the morning, I arrived at my new friend's house for a turkey hunt on his place. This was my first trip, having only recently met him through one of my deacons.

After talking a bit too long, we had to hurry to our hunting spot. The purported quarter mile turned into a five-mile hike, but that wasn't the wonder.

As we descended a logging road, I was overwhelmed by the height of the "little hills" that turned into sheer cliffs, but that wasn't the wonder.

When we located the first gobbling bird of the morning, the wonder materialized. I looked over at my new buddy and watched in amazement as he put on his camouflage head net.

"So, what's the wonder?" I just knew you would ask. Part of the wonder was the head net he was struggling to put over his head. It consisted of the bottom portion of the leg of a former "pair" of camoflauge pants. Only the eye holes altered the original equipment, but that wasn't the wonder either.

The true wonder of the day finally evolved, but took a little time to develop. As we sat as quietly and as still as possible, waiting for the gobbler to make his amorous arrival, said hunting buddy began to get a bit restless. He didn't have a tired tube, just a tired...seat.

Presently, a hen meandered up. Her entrance was from behind the pant-headed partner, thus preventing him from recognizing that the turkey was a she-bird.

The nervous neophyte(his first turkey hunt ever!) commenced to quiver just a bit with the excitement of the moment. Then he began to tremble ever so slightly. Finally, when the bird wouldn't come out where he could see her, he started to shake all over.

As I tried to control my own quivering, I observed the true wonder of the morning. There it was in plain view, for all the world to see.

A full-grown man succeeded in causing a likewise full-grown oak tree to quiver, then tremble, and finally shake so violently that leaves began to disembark and dead limbs fall violently to the ground.

With such a wonder to behold, the hen wheeled and walked off, not clucking as she had arrived, but chuckling!

My, my, my. Wonders never cease to be!

Turkey hunting with a pants-headed buddy might be a long shot for you, but...

Whatever you do, don't be afraid to go with the long shots. Live life to its fullest every moment and be ready!

"Do not be deceived: "Evil company corrupts good habits."
(I Corinthians 15:33)

THE COMPANY WE KEEP

As you see from the above scripture, the Bible says that the company we keep has a direct impact on our values. Without a doubt, this is a true statement, but one has to have good morals to begin with before there's a danger of them being corrupted.

Where do get our morals? Where do we get such things as manners, politeness, kindness, obedience? Let me suggest that we get our ideas about morality and ethics from our families, our churches, and those with whom we are closely associated, in other words, our friends.

You may be thinking, "Oh no, this is going to be a sermon instead of a chapter in an outdoor book." Well, whoa there, partner. Give me a minute before you unload and give up on this long shot.

On a trip to the Southeastern Outdoor Press Association's annual meeting in Lake Charles, Louisiana, a few years back, I was blessed with more than the great hospitality of the people of southwestern Louisiana, and by more than their fantastic Cajun cooking.

It was my pleasure to meet Mr. Dave Hall, the chief law enforcement officer with the U.S. Fish and Wildlife Service. While sharing some thoughts on the preservation of our natural resources through ethical hunting, he mentioned a federal judge in Alaska who had made a very interesting and telling comment. The judge told Dave Hall, "I've never had a youth before me in court who had a hunting/fishing license in his wallet."

What was the judge saying? He was saying that those young people with parents who love their children enough to get them out from in front of the T.V. and into the woods or out on the lake are rarely in trouble with the law.

Young people who grow up hunting and fishing, backpacking and camping, loving to photograph or artistically reproduce the flora and fauna of our world tend to have manners. They are polite. They tend to become gentle and kind, considerate, and above all productive, law-abiding citizens.

Why do young people who are introduced to the great outdoors early in life tend to be the kind of people you want for your neighbors? Well, I really believe it's the company they keep.

Parents are certainly the first of that number. As we get older, the people we're around at deer camp or in the bass club are added to the list of the company we keep. We begin to learn that our state and federal game wardens aren't riding around trying to catch people so much as trying to preserve our sporting opportunities. They're teaching hunter education courses and are out there restocking lakes with fish and wilderness areas with game animals such as the incredibly successful wild turkey program here in Mississippi. They're conducting research efforts at Mississippi State University, as well as enforcing game laws.

People our own age who also enjoy the same outdoor sports we do start to enhance our list of friends. In a few short years, we've surrounded ourselves with a company of people who create an environment in which outdoor morality and ethics are a way of life.

Besides the people we meet through our outdoor experiences, there are others who help us build and maintain a moral and ethical environment, especially as that relates to hunting and fishing. Who are they? The first squirrel, dove, duck, turkey, or deer seen in the wild becomes part of the company we keep. As youngsters, we watch in awe as deer demonstrate how to be alert for danger, how to communicate effectively with others of its species, how to deal with conflict, hunger, and survival.

These friends teach us many lessons. The first time a young

person takes one of these friends with a rifle or shotgun, something very emotional happens. A wave of both elation and sadness floods the soul. The creature held by tiny hands is more beautiful than we ever imagined. Even a gray squirrel seems to have a majestic beauty during this moment of truth.

When the first blood is drawn by a young hunter or fisherman, the company we keep becomes more important than ever. Will this youth become a blood-thirsty, law-breaking game hog or poacher, or will he or she be blessed with a parent or mentor who will take the time to explain game management and the role man plays in keeping the food chain balanced?

Even though there are those who think that man should be strictly vegetarian, I, for one, believe that we are here on this earth to rule over it wisely and subdue it for the glory of God and our enjoyment. We have a responsibility to manage our resources through sound game management practices in order to preserve our wildlife and our outdoor recreational sports.

Clearly, the company we keep is extremely important to the future of hunting, fishing, and the survival of our native wildlife.

Preserving our outdoor sports of hunting, fishing, or just strolling the woods among the wildlife we know today may be a long shot, but...

Whatever you do, don't be afraid to go with the long shots. Live life to its fullest every moment and be ready!

"Every one of them is gone back: they are altogether become filthy; there is none that does good, no, not one." (Psalms 53:3)

TRASH, TRASH, AND MORE TRASH

Picking up trash carelessly discarded by thoughtless people is not my idea of fun. Through the Adopt-A-Highway Program and involvement with local service organizations, I've picked up everything from aluminum cans to baby diapers on the side of the highway. If nothing else has come of these activities, I have learned how important it is to dispose of trash properly. The side of the road is no place for our garbage!

Being the pastor of a small-town church has provided me with other opportunities to deal with trash. Just about every Saturday night, people riding around in obviously festive moods deposit at least one or two beer cans or bottles around our church. It's a delicate operation for the parson to be walking down the sidewalk early Sunday morning with an empty beer can in his hand when a deacon from the Baptist Church drives by! My thanks to those who leave these mementos which have to be picked up before Sunday services each week.

Besides the church yard, one would also think that the woods is another place where trash shouldn't be found. But alas, it's not so. All too often a casual stroll through the woods is spoiled by the aggravating sight of someone's coke can or candy wrappers.

Just like trash on the roadside, you never know what you'll see walking through the woods. Some days a plastic garbage bag wouldn't be sufficient to hold it all. It amazes me to no end to see what people will carelessly discard in the woods.

God has given us a beautiful and wondrous gift in the great outdoors. The places on this planet where we can go and experience some peace and quiet are so limited. It's a crying shame when someone trashes this great gift.

Risking the wrath of hunters and fishermen who may read this, I want to suggest that each of us bring at least one piece of trash home with us the next time we go to the lake or the woods. If each of us would start doing something to improve the environment by picking up a can or a bottle or a plastic candy wrapper each time we go out, pretty soon the slobs who keep trashing the place will wake up and cut it out! Those of you who enjoy a peaceful early morning or late-evening walk through the streets can do the same for your pretty little town or awesomely large city.

Years ago, when we were living down in rural Smith County, Mississippi, garbage dumps were a real problem. There were no landfills or regular garbage pick-ups out in the county, so most folks just hunted up a gully to throw their trash in. One of our church members who lived a short distance from our house woke up one morning to discover that someone had thrown trash in the ditch in front of his home. Angered by the unsightly and smelly garbage, the man of the house picked up every piece of the garbage and in the process discovered a letter with the offending party's name and address. He sacked up the mess and returned every bit of it that evening.

Next morning, he gave the person a call. "Did you get your package?" he asked.

"What package?"

"The package that fell out of your truck in front of my house?"

Click.

No doubt, I hope, that person was embarrassed and a whole lot wiser than before. Let me encourage each of us to properly dispose of trash. Don't unwrap that candy and throw the paper in someone's yard or on the street. Don't pitch that can on the side of the highway, or in the woods, or in the church yard either! God has given us a great world in which to live. Let's stop trashing the place!

Disposing of your trash and garbage properly may be a long shot for you, but...

Whatever you do, don't be afraid to go with the long shots. Live life to its fullest every moment and be ready!

111

"The kingdom of heaven is like a merchant seeking beautiful pearls, who, when he had found one pearl of great price, went and sold all that he had and bought it."   (Matthew 13:46)

CHECK IT OUT!

A good hunter is one who knows the value of pre-season scouting and practices the same. A good writer is one who has keen powers of observation and uses them. Given the above definitions of a good hunter and a good writer, I must admit failure on both counts, but I'm working on them.

This past week, Red Solomon, retired owner of "Y-D Lumber Company, Belzoni, Mississippi, where you save money," mentioned a really fine snowshoe hare video he had checked out from our local library. Shamefaced, I listened to Red as he related the thrill of the hunt as recorded on this fine piece of video. Why was I ashamed? Because I've never gone into our local library and checked out their outdoor video section!

Determined not only to see the error of my ways but make amends, I went down to the Humphreys County Library and began to browse and ask questions. It shouldn't surprise those of you who frequent your local library to hear that our librarians, Mrs. Keenum and Mrs. Rodgers, were thrilled to show me around and answer my questions. Magdalene Gammil and Joanne Abney, their able assistants, were also there ready to help those who aren't too familiar with using a card catalog or with finding a particular type of book, magazine, or video which might be of interest.

Our local libraries are a treasure that more of us should dig into. With some 800 videos in our small-town library, we have just about anything of a decent nature that us locals might want to look at. Naturally, I went looking for hunting and fishing videos of which there are some 25-30.

The hunter/fisherman/trapper can go in and check out such videos as Dave Embry's "Monster Bucks" or "Stalking the Gray Ghost," or Will Primos' "Truth" videos on turkey hunting. There are videos about trapping beavers, minks, and raccoons, bass fishing(I think our local bass club president must be watching these), bears, hogs, and snowshoe hare hunting.

For nature lovers, the ones that just want to observe and admire, there are videos about bears(not just Pooh Bear either), Bengal tigers, bald eagles, and whitetail deer. These wonderful videos contain breathtaking scenes and are well worth the time to sit and watch.

Sorry to say, the books on hunting don't seem to be checked out nearly as often as the videos. Kind of sad, isn't it? Why's it sad? Because it means that those I wish to inspire to go down and use the library might not be reading this either!

In any event, they have a great selection of books by people like Robert Ruark and Zane Grey. They have children's books on animals and hunting as well. <u>A Boy and His Gun</u> by E.C. Janes is one that comes highly recommended. If you go to the card catalog in your nearby library and check under the heading "Hunting," you'll uncover a good many gems. If you check under "Hunting-Humorous Stories," you'll find a fine book by the title, <u>Tired Tubes and Ten-Speed Turkeys</u>. If it isn't there, it ought to be, so ask for it!

The day I was there, I checked out <u>Tall Timber Gabriels</u> by Charles Whittington, a bow hunting delight by Saxton Pope, and one on deer hunting by Russell Tinsley. They were superb, so hurry down to your nearest public library before all the videos and books get checked out.

Magazines are also available for you to peruse while you're there. They should have such publications as "Delta Wildlife," which is published by the Delta Wildlife Foundation here in Mississippi, "National Wildlife" and "International Wildlife," which are published by the National Wildlife Federation, and others. For the tree-huggers, they also have "Sierra," which is published by the Sierra Club. There's something for every person at every age right next door in our libraries. Check it out!

I truly hope that making use of your local library hasn't been a long shot for you, but even if it has...

Whatever you do, don't be afraid to go with the long shots. Live life to its fullest every moment and be ready!

"Come to Me, all you who labor and are heavy laden, and I will give you rest. Take My yoke upon you and learn from Me, for I am gentle and lowly in heart, and you will find rest for your souls. For My yoke is easy and My burden is light." (Matthew 11:28-30)

THE FAMILY VACATION

Taken your annual family vacation yet? Lots of folks take vacations every summer. In fact, as I write about this wonderful subject, the Wiman family is on vacation, checking out the Atlanta Braves, Stone Mountain, Six Flags over Georgia, and many other sordid(I mean "assorted") sights and sounds of the Peach state's capital.

Every time I go on a vacation, I come back wondering why it's called a vacation. I'm always so completely exhausted after a vacation that I need a vacation before going back to work! As a result of my own personal experience with vacations, I decided to do a little research into the subject.

For example, I discovered that our word, "vacation," comes from the Latin "vacare," which means "to be empty." To "vacate" means to be unoccupied, thus when we go on vacation, we empty our place of work and home and leave for a while.

Webster's Dictionary tells us that a vacation is "freedom from any activity; rest; respite; intermission: a period of rest and freedom from work, study, etc.; time of recreation, usually a specific interval in a year..."

Measured by such a definition, I don't think I've had too many vacations in my lifetime. I had a few when I was young, but my parents didn't.

Most vacations begin very early in the morning, while it's

cool outside and the traffic isn't too heavy. Sleepy kids are led to the car with their pillows in hand, and away you go!

After about two hours or so, one little voice after another begins to sing the same song, "Dad, when are we gonna stop? I gotta go."

After another thirty minutes or so, one larger voice joins the growing chorus, "Honey, when ARE we gonna stop? I gotta go, too."

Some ten minutes later, amidst threats of car-jacking, assault, divorce, murder(this is the sordid part I mentioned earlier), we stop at a roadside park or Welcome Center for the needed break.

What is it about women needing "to go" anyway? And what is it about men who think they have to drive ten straight hours without stopping to reach a place nobody is in a hurry to get to anyway? As one adept counselor put it, "Men are into conquering, and on a vacation, the road happens to be what needs conquering..."

It's sad that most of us men don't realize the value of stopping along the way to admire the scenery, smell the roses, dip the toes in a mountain stream, or take a few minutes to enjoy the shade and feel the gentle caress of a summer's breeze. Life would be much sweeter, vacations much more enjoyable, and our marriages would probably survive at a greater rate than they presently do if we would act more like a sponge and less like sand paper on our vacations.

Truth is, vacations with the family are fun. At least, they can be. Watching the children laugh and have a ball, watching the wife not have to cook or wash dishes, not worrying about the phone ringing incessantly, day and night, are what vacations are all about.

A few days on a far-away lake with some of your buddies, or a week in November at the deer camp, or a few days in the spring chasing wild turkeys are mighty good vacations in my book, but taking the family on a vacation for a few days shouldn't be a long shot. It ought to be a sure shot, but...

Whatever you do, don't be afraid to go with the long shots. Live life to its fullest every moment and be ready!

115

"He who dwells in the secret place of the Most High shall abide under the shadow of the Almighty. I will say of the Lord, `He is my refuge and my fortress; my God, in Him I will trust.' Surely He shall deliver you from the snare of the fowler and from the perilous pestilence. He shall cover you with His feathers, and under His wings you shall take refuge; His truth shall be your shield and buckler. You shall not be afraid of the terror by night, nor of the arrow that flies by day, nor of the pestilence that walks in darkness, nor of the destruction that lays waste at noonday."(Psalms 91:1-6)

DANGER IN THE DEEP WOODS

This particular "Long Shots" will take a different approach from the usual combination of poignant pictures and hilariously humorous stories you're used to. Bear with me as we look at a very serious situation, a potentially life-threatening situation.

Test your knowledge a bit, will you? Can you name the fastest growing infectious disease in the United States today? If you said, "Aids," you're correct and on top of what's happening in your world.

Here's a tougher question. Can you name the second fastest growing infectious disease in America today? Not sure? This is a tough one. Let me give you a couple of hints.

Most people associate this disease with hunters. Still not sure? Okay then, one more hint ought to do it. It's name is the same as that of a small, green, lemon-shaped fruit. If you said, "Lyme Disease," you guessed it.

Maybe it's hard to believe, or maybe you've never even heard of Lyme Disease, but it's a very dangerous tick-borne disease. The Centers for Disease Control(CDC) reported a 17% increase in cases of Lyme Disease in 1991. Many researchers and observers believe that only one in ten cases are being reported.

Who is at risk of developing Lyme Disease? You are, if you work in your backyard or garden between April and October and when temperatures are above 40 degrees Fahrenheit.

You are at risk if you are a pet owner, because your dog or cat may bring ticks into your house from the yard. You are at risk if you

116

hunt, fish, hike, play golf, or camp. Your children are at risk if they spend time playing outside during the spring and summer months. You are at risk if your profession requires you to work outside.

Lyme Disease, if not properly diagnosed and treated can be fatal, which is exactly what happened to a relative of one of our church members during the fall of 1992. Tommy Pitner was bitten by an infected tick Labor Day weekend of that year and died within a month of complications from the disease. In this young man's experience, the worst case scenario was played out. For the vast majority of cases, however, Lyme Disease can be successfully treated with antibiotics.

What are the symptoms? Though there are over 200 possible symptoms, the disease usually develops in three stages.

In the first thirty days, a rash occurs, the most prevalent of which is the bull's eye rash. In addition, fatigue, stiffness of the neck, muscle aches and pains, and flu-like symptoms may be observed.

In the second stage, after a month or more, heart palpitations, shortness of breath, fainting, irregular heartbeats, paralysis of facial nerves, chest pain, loss of appetite, hearing loss, meningitis, and encephalitis may result.

After several months, chronic Lyme Disease symptoms may include swollen and painful joints and other arthritic symptoms, heart blocks, depression, memory loss, blindness, and symptoms mimicking multiple sclerosis may also be experienced.

Left untreated, the disease will systematically attack every internal organ in the body. As the old saying goes, "An ounce of prevention is worth a pound of cure." So take precautions against Lyme Disease.

Here are a few common sense suggestions to help protect yourself from contracting this dangerous disease.

1. Avoid grassy and marshy woodland areas.

2. Don't walk barefoot through grassy areas.

3. Stay on established trails, avoiding contact with possible tick-infested shrubs.

4. Wear light-colored shirts with long sleeves and long pants. Tuck shirts into pants and pants into socks or boots.

5. Wear a light-colored hat(it's easy to see ticks on light-colored clothing).

6. Always check carefully for ticks when you come home from an outdoor trip.

7. Use an insect repellent with DEET as its main ingredient.

Though there are many good products on the market, I would suggest using Repel products such as "Repel Tick Kit" or "Repel Insect Repellent for Sportsman or Family."

If you engage in any type outdoor activity or profession, be aware of the very real danger of Lyme Disease. Use caution. Be careful. Know the symptoms of the disease. Stay healthy.

Avoiding ticks in our hot and humid environment may be a long shot for the outdoor enthusiast, but...

Whatever you do, don't be afraid to go with the long shots. Live life to its fullest every moment and be ready!

In the fall of the year...

"And these words which I command you today shall be in your heart; you shall teach them diligently to your children, and shall talk of them when you sit in your house, when you walk by the way, when you lie down, and when you rise up. You shall bind them as a sign on your hand, and they shall be as frontlets between your eyes. You shall write them on the doorposts of your house and on your gates."(Deuteronomy 6:6-9)

NATIONAL HUNTING AND FISHING DAY

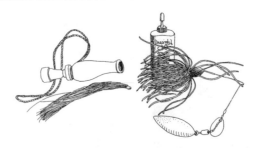

The fourth Saturday in September is usually the day set aside to observe National Hunting and Fishing Day. All across America, people will be out hunting and fishing and enjoying what God has given us in the land of plenty, but very few will take the time to tell a non-hunter or non-fisherman about the importance of our outdoor life and the incredible opportunities to hunt, fish, or just plain enjoy the flora and fauna of our great nation.

When the first settlers came over from Europe, they encountered native Americans who knew what they had and made wise use of the land and its wildlife. Europeans, however, didn't come equipped with the same respect for game animals and fish that the Indians had developed.

As a result of increasing populations, lack of game laws or management plans, and habitat losses, the numbers of huntable animals diminished rather rapidly. By the early 1800's, with the growing demand for meat and fish outstripping the ability of ranchers and commercial fishermen to supply that demand, market hunting became an accepted practice. The passenger pigeon was hunted into extinction, and with westward expansion, the buffalo almost "flew the coup" with the pigeon.

By the turn of the century, many of America's large game animals were in serious decline. The numbers of buffalo were down to nothing. Whitetail and mule deer, elk, and wild turkey were also in trouble in many areas of the land.

Today we're hearing a whole lot from animal rights groups about the need to ban hunting and fishing all together in order to preserve our game animals from extinction. The idea of game management without hunting isn't new.

One of America's most popular Presidents and a very avid hunter, Theodore Roosevelt, attempted to manage the elk population on the Kaibab Plateau, part of the Grand Canyon National Park, by closing it to hunting for a number of years. His idea was to "preserve" the elk population by reducing the numbers being killed. Even predator populations were reduced.

For a number of years the elk population increased just as intended. As a result of the increased numbers though, one winter there wasn't enough food for all the elk. They ate the browse down to the point that the foliage didn't grow back the next spring. Cowboys were hired to drive the elk to greener pastures, but even the weakest eluded the drivers to return to the foodless areas. Over the next couple of years, the numbers of elk lost to starvation and disease were enormous.

Wildlife officials learned the hard way that game such as deer and turkey can't be preserved. They must be managed through conservation and habitat improvement. Hunting and fishing are tools in the conservation and management of our wild game and fish populations.

Thanks to the foresight and generosity of hunters and fishermen, nearly $400 billion has come into federal and state coffers for acquisition of wetlands, establishment of wildlife refuges, wildlife restoration projects like the wild turkey in Mississippi, and the passage of legislation intended to make hunting and fishing safer(Hunter Education courses for example).

By contrast, the tree-huggers and animal rights groups have failed miserably to do anything except make lots of noise and gain the ear of the liberal media. In a rare moment of honesty, four such individuals, speaking to the Outdoor Writers Association of

America in Portland, Oregon, admitted that their goals are to outlaw all hunting and fishing. Two of the four fessed up that they believe that all of us should be vegetarians. During the summer months, I dearly love a plate full of peas, beans, fresh creamed corn and ruby-red tomatoes. After a meal or two of nothing but veggies, I'm once again ready for a delicious deer steak, fried quail or a slab of white perch.

When the National Hunting and Fishing Day comes round, give some thought to the blessings we enjoy today because of the great outdoors. Hunting and fishing may be a long shot for you, but... Whatever you do, don't be afraid to go with the long shots. Live life to its fullest every moment and be ready!

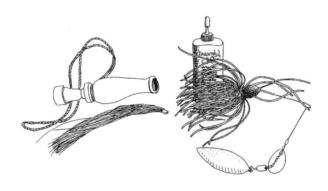

"My soul, wait silently for God alone, for my expectation is from Him."(Psalms 62:5)

ANTICIPATION

Anticipation—what Webster defines as "expectation," is often more thrilling than the actual event. Sometimes the anticipation of a coming attraction is so charged with excitement and promise that the event itself doesn't measure up.

For example, in early September each year the first dove season of the hunting year opens. That first Saturday in September in the Deep South marks the beginning of the year for many outdoorsmen, of far greater significance and causing much more anticipation than New Year's Day ever will.

Around our house, anticipation is the word. The old shotgun is caught up in the throes of anticipation. Locked away since last winter, the dusty, dirty weapon is eagerly anticipating a thorough cleaning. It sure needs one!

Out in the kennel, the aging lab is also caught up in the anticipation of Opening Day. When the weather suddenly turns unseasonably cool a week or so before the season opens, as it nearly always does, she starts getting real frisky. She seems to know that dove season is fast approaching, which means a reprieve from the confinement of concrete and chain link fence. Just the anticipation of a few days in the field with her hunting partner always gives her a burst of energy. Though gray around the mouth and feet and suffering from arthritis, opening day still gives her the adrenaline to jump into the back of the Toyota for that ear-flapping, tongue-flopping, tail-wagging ride to the hunt.

Out in the storeroom/closet/hunting lair, anticipation is running rampant as well. Camo clothing, reloading equipment, and special dove hunting paraphernalia seem to get caught up in the excitement of the approach of Opening Day.

The clothing is anticipating the washing they should have received last spring before they were hastily put away after the close of turkey season. The empty shotgun shell hulls eagerly wait to be reloaded—at the last minute. Why do I always wait until 10:00 on Friday night to remember that I don't have any shells for the early hunt on Saturday morning? The cooler, water jug, and special stools are also filled with the anticipation that drips like heavy mist from the atmosphere, the anticipation of being dragged out at the last minute and thrown into the back of the truck for the short ride to the dove field.

The mailman is even caught up in the anticipation of Opening Day. He's expecting delivery of that last-minute order of some new item from the latest catalog. The advertisement said it was guaranteed to work like a charm, that no hunt is complete without it. "How did you ever make it without it?" was the spousal comment when I said I HAD to call the 800 number and get it shipped overnight in order to have it for Opening Day.

The children are also filled with anticipation. They want to know if they'll get to go on their first hunt. "Which shotgun do I get to use? Do I have to sit right beside you, Dad, or do I get to sit by myself this year?" Can you feel the anticipation?

In the midst of all this anticipation, I'm about to explode with excitement myself. I'm wondering how I can hunt with everybody who's already invited me. I'm wondering how I'm going to manage to hunt with three young ladies, at least one of whom always needs to leave the field and go to the house for a minute.

As the time draws nearer and nearer for Opening Day, my anticipation blossoms into dreams. If all goes as it has in the past, I'll get to bed about 11:00 the night before. As soon as my head hits the pillow, I'll begin to see visions, clouds of doves swarming into the sunflower field at daylight.

There will be shouts from other hunters, "Comin' your way, Preacher!" I'll stay seated until the last possible second, and then in one fluid motion rise to my feet, shoulder the little 20 gauge Remington 1100, swing on the first bird of the season, squeeze the

124

trigger, and realize with a sudden jolt, which shakes the entire bed, that I forgot to load the stupid thing—again!

I'll slip back into a deep sleep after the awakening shock of the dream, and soon envision the same scene. This time, as I squeeze the trigger, a whole flock of doves fall to a single shot. As I pick up the incredible results of my first shot of the season(at least twenty birds), a game warden taps me on the shoulder. BOOM! I'm awake again with another jolt to the bed (the daily limit for doves is fifteen). By this time, Dorothy is about ready for me to take my anticipation to the couch so she can get some sleep!

Anticipation—can be exciting, dream inspiring, even frustrating. Anticipating the Opening Day of dove season might be a long shot for you, but...

Whatever you do, don't be afraid to go with the long shots. Live life to its fullest every moment and be ready!

"Out of the depths I have cried to You, O Lord; Lord, hear my voice! Let Your ears be attentive to the voice of my supplications."(Psalms 130:1-2)

SPLISH SPLASH

Water has many uses. We drink it, wash ourselves, our clothes, and our cars with it. We swim and fish in it, and baptize with it.

When water gets in short supply, as it did one spring, Christian churches had to cut down just like everybody else. I heard it got so dry out in Texas a couple of years ago that the Baptists had to sprinkle. The Methodists used a damp rag, and the Presbyterians gave rain checks!

Like I was saying, water has many uses. On our local golf course, water plays an important role in a number of ways. When it's hot and dry, the sprinkler system keeps the fairways and greens alive.

Besides providing life to dry grass, water plays a devilish role of sorts on a couple of holes. Running alongside the fifth hole is the cut-off of the Yazoo River. The Indians sure knew what they were doing when they named this waterway the "river of death," because it continues to be death to many a golf ball on the fifth hole of the country club.

On the sixth hole, a couple of strategically-placed ponds, separated from the fairway on this hole by a levee, come into play as you tee off. When they come into play, I usually get TEED OFF sure enough!

Recently, I was playing a round of golf with a local x-ray technician(un-named but not unknown to many locals). My tee shot didn't find the water, but it almost did. The sphere came to rest on the cart path that runs along the base of the levee.

Said x-ray tech drove me down the levee and descended to the cart path so I could hit my next shot. As I turned away from the golf cart, the designated driver(a role his friends say he isn't used to filling) started back up the levee, but developed a problem.

Golf carts don't climb straight up levees very well. The wheels started spinning and the cart started sliding—backwards. In a flash, the speed of descent was far in excess of the anticipated speed of ascent.

Reacting as quickly as possible, the golf cart charioteer bailed out leaving the careening cart cascading down the levee toward the pond. This sea captain was not going nobly down with his ship.

From behind me came a rumbling, thundering thud. The earth shook, and I wheeled about to see my partner struggling to regain his feet, flailing his hands in the air, yelling mild obscenities and pointing at an object that I suddenly realized was our cart.

What a sight! The golf cart, with our clubs partially submerged, resting peacefully in three feet of muddy, murky water. "Ole buddy," I said with a smirk and a sigh of mock disgust, "You Baptists will go to any `links' to get us Presbyterians immersed!"

The possibility of your seeing a partially immersed golf cart during your next round of golf may be a long shot, but...

Whatever you do, don't be afraid to go with the long shots. Live life to its fullest every moment and be ready!

"Behold, I tell you a mystery . . ."(I Corinthians 15:51a)

A STRANGE STORY TELLER

I met a strange story teller the other day—my truck. After the close of deer season, I had the red "Toytoy" serviced and washed. A clean Toyota 4/WD was such a strange sight that our little York-a-Poo, Fuzzy, didn't even recognize the strange vehicle in the carport the next morning and put up quite a fuss. Tells you how long it had been since the thing had been washed, doesn't it?

Feeling quite proud of the clean conveyance, I parked it near the door of the church Sunday evening. Would you believe it? An otherwise sweet lady in our church came in and said, "Your truck sure is dirty."

"What? I just had the thing washed! What do you mean dirty?"

Elizabeth Snooty(her nickname to some, but not her real name) was referring to all the trash in the bed of the truck.
Well, she was right. I looked over in the back, and it was filthy, but as the old saying goes, "One man's junk is another man's treasure." As I gazed into the truck bed, it began to tell a story.

I saw a piece of rope that reminded me of the day that Ruth, Joy, and I put up some deer stands for the three of us to use. That was three months earlier.

There was a short piece of 2X4 board that spoke of the night we had a fire-building contest at the Boy Scout meeting. All the little sticks recalled the camping trip back in November, which happened to be the only cold weather we had until January rolled around. Troop 91 never goes camping unless it rains or turns freezing cold—or both!

My aged lab, Kelly, came to mind as I saw a plastic bucket

128

peeking out from under the tool box. She had sucked the bottom out of it trying to cool down on a September dove hunt. Yes, she found and retrieved all fifteen birds I shot that opening morning.

There were some aluum(alumnium to some) cans and a large bag to put them in to help keep the scout troop financially sound. By the way folks, if you see a beer can or two in the back of my truck, they're not mine!

The bag of empty shotgun shell hulls reminded me of the squirrel hunt that had been so much fun. They also reminded me that I needed to reload a couple of boxes before next season.

The jumper cables, anti-freeze, and old water pump brought back some not-so-pleasant memories of the week it was Monday every day.

The set of deer horns and another piece of rope told a story of hunts that did and didn't put any meat on the table. I rattled the horns as per instructions on the video tape, but to no avail. The piece of rope helped load a deer when no one else was around to help on another occasion.

As you can see, story tellers come in strange forms and at times when you least expect them to pop up. The red 1982 Toyota pick-up carried me over 200,000 miles before giving way to a newer model. Who knows? There may be many new tales for the 4 Runner to tell.

The very thought of a hunting truck being a story teller might be a long shot, but...

Whatever you do, don't be afraid to go with the long shots. Live life to its fullest every moment and be ready!

"Among all these people there were seven hundred select men who were left-handed; every one could sling a stone at a hair's breadth and not miss."(Judges 20:16)

COTTONTAIL TALES

Rabbit hunting is in full swing these days, but it seems as though good beagles, plentiful rabbits, and opportunities to go hunting are scarce.

One of the finest gentlemen who hunts rabbits in these parts called the other evening. "We're gonna meet at my house about eight in the morning. You're welcome to join us."

Knowing how disappointed everyone would be if I didn't show up, I thanked my host for the invitation and hung up the phone.

"Who was that, dear?" the wife asked.

"It was Sam"

"Sam who?"

"Sam, the premier rabbit hunter of Humphreys County."

"What did he want?"

"Wanted to know if I thought he ought to take a short position on pork bellies when the market opens Monday morning."

"What time did he say to meet him to go rabbit hunting," she asked with that sadistic, all-knowing chuckle that all hunting wives seem to possess.

Doesn't it bug you that your wife knows what the other party says when you're talking on the phone, and asks the question anyway?

About 8:00 next morning, vehicles with tags from Hinds, Attala, Sunflower, Holmes, and Humphreys County began pulling into Sam's driveway. Before long, between hunters, beagles, and children, we had a three-ring circus going on. "We better get out of here before Mickey gets after us with her shotgun!"

We pooled rides as much as possible, but the departing rabbit hunters looked like a middle eastern caravan. The short drive to a long drainage canal proved to be the right choice for the day. The wet cutover timber that was our other choice would have been tough, what with house-high briar patches, standing water, and downed tree tops everywhere.

The hunt was great. The fifteen or so beagles, with their ringing cries after the bunnies, made bark fly off trees. Ten rabbits were very cooperative, allowing the beagles to chase them round and round before passing within gun range of the hunters.

A goodly number wound up in the pot in several homes the next week. Fried rabbit, rice and gravy, homemade biscuits and molasses are hard to beat.

But the best part of all was the fun we had laughing at each other's jokes and kidding each other about all the misses(not to be confused with the Mrs. who seem to know our minds). "Howard can't hit 'em up close. He has to let 'em get on out there far enough for his eyes to focus before he can hit 'em." We all hooted at Ole Fuzz, who was good-natured enough to laugh along with the joke told on him.

The comradery's the best part, don't ya see? Even if you don't see, and rabbit hunting is a long shot for you...

Don't be afraid to go with the long shots. Live life to its fullest every moment and be ready!

"A man's heart plans his way, but the Lord directs his steps."(Proverbs 16:9)

THE BEST LAID PLANS

Sometimes it just doesn't pay to plan. Normally, I can't stand to do anything without a well thought out plan, but there are times when "the best laid plans" fall through.

The other evening, I was watching a high school basketball game when one of my former Eagle Scouts, a pre-med student at Ole Miss, sat down beside me to visit.

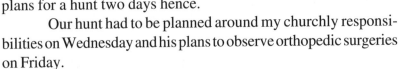

From personal matters of grades and love life, the conversation turned to our common interest in deer hunting. We agreed that the 1991-92 season was the worst we'd seen in all our years(mine many more than his!). Our lack of prior success didn't deter us from making plans for a hunt two days hence.

Our hunt had to be planned around my churchly responsibilities on Wednesday and his plans to observe orthopedic surgeries on Friday.

Knowing about my bad knee, he said, "Maybe I'll get to watch the surgeon work on you." Little did we know that his words weren't far from being fulfilled.

As I stood to go introduce the starting line-ups for the boys' basketball game, a sharp pain rippled down from my left knee toward my shin. Quickly, I resumed my seat and began rubbing the offending joint.

Once more I stood to proceed to the scorer's table. No good. PAIN!

Two days later, the same Thursday which was supposed to be our hunt, I was sitting in the office of the very same surgeon we had discussed.

After explaining my pain and the suddenness with which it came on, the doctor ordered a series of x-rays and other tests.

His conclusion was that I'm getting old. Can you believe that? I'm a very young 40+ years, for heaven's sake.

It seems that the combination of two previous surgeries, a few too many pounds, a few too few exercises, and the growing presence of Arthur Rightis have brought the inevitable and sure sign of age...aches and pains in the joints.

I still hope we can go on that hunt one of these days, though I will preface it with pain pills, an ice pack for an hour or so, and a knee sleeve.

We just can't allow aches or pains or the dead of winter to keep us deer hunters from firing our appointed rounds, can we? Killing a nice buck in spite of the groaning of an old man with a bad knee might be a long shot, but I'm willing to take it. What about you? Not afraid of a little long shot, are you? Even if you are...

Don't be afraid to go with the long shots. Live life to its fullest every moment and be ready!

"Thus I establish My covenant with you: Never again shall all flesh be cut off by the waters of the flood; never again shall there be a flood to destroy the earth." And God said: 'This is the sign of the covenant which I make between Me and you, and every living creature that is with you, for perpetual generations: I set My rainbow in the cloud, and it shall be for the sign of the covenant between Me and the earth. It shall be, when I bring a cloud over the earth, that the rainbow shall be seen in the cloud; and I will remember My covenant which is between Me and you and every living creature of all flesh; the waters shall never again become a flood to destroy all flesh. The rainbow shall be in the cloud, and I will look on it to remember the everlasting covenant between God and every living creature of all flesh that is on the earth.' And God said to Noah, 'This is the sign of the covenant which I have established between Me and all flesh that is on the earth.' "

(I Kings 22:31-33)

WET, AIN'T IT?

Wet, ain't it? It's September and time for the traditional dry weather of the harvest season, but it's mighty wet. First, hurricane Andrew blew through, soaking our part of the world. Then, exactly a week later, a strong cold front came barrelling down on us from the northwest. The lightning was brilliant, awesome actually, but the downpours; well...wet, ain't it?

When things get wet, it can be mighty disagreeable. For weeks now, some of our outdoor enthusiasts have been nursing their carefully and legally prepared fields for the opening of dove season. When it gets this wet, the birds get scattered all over the countryside and, you might say, it "dampens" the spirits of the hunt organizers and the hunters counting the days until the season opens.

Yep, when things get wet, it can be mighty disagreeable. As the local folks know, the Presbyterian Church in Belzoni is located on the corner of Church and Pecan Streets. This particular corner

134

is a low spot that turns into a lake when sudden and heavy showers inundate the community.

Such was the case the other Wednesday. The trained voices of the chancel choir were melodiously practicing when lightning flashed and thunder rumbled through, rattling the 75-year-old stained-glass windows. Unbeknownst to the singers within, a sure enough rain was falling outside.

When we left practice, one fine Lincoln was, as Kermit the Frog would put it, "knee deep" in the temporary lake. Being the gentleman that I am, I volunteered to wade out and retrieve the vehicle from the watery depository.

Barefoot with britches legs rolled up, amidst all kinds of hoots and cat calls, I sloshed out and got in. Water was ankle deep inside the car! It took several more minutes after reaching higher ground to bail out the excess muddy water.

Yep, when things get wet, it can be mighty disagreeable. I remember a couple of incidents from my college duck-hunting days that illustrate how disagreeable wet can be.

My hunting buddies and I had built a really nice blind out in Pelahatchie Bay on Barnett Reservoir, just outside Jackson. After hiding the boat under some brush, it was a short wade through hip-deep water to the blind. Three closely placed steps up, and we were concealed in our hide-away and ready to ambush some ducks.

One bitterly cold morning, a guest of mine dropped a mallard, and being on the side closest to the only exit (dumb move on my part to sit in that spot!), I started to back out so I could climb down and retrieve the downed(would you believe, no pun intended?) duck.

Well, graceful applies to deer and dear wives, but definitely not to me in a pair of waders. With one foot on the top step, I hung the heel of my other wader-clad foot on the edge of the door jam and yep, casploosh!

I was up in a flash, much to the astonishment of my partners, both of whom were suddenly overcome by a strong desire to cough and clear their throats. When water is below 40 degrees, and the wind is whipping the 30 degree air at a 20 mile per hour clip right out of Santa's storehouse, wet can be mighty disagreeable. Needless to say, we had a choice between burning up the blind or a short hunt. We opted for the short hunt.

On another one of those cold, miserable January days, I was wading ashore from another duck blind. We were hunting in a new spot, with which I was unfamiliar.

The hunt that morning had been a real flop, but the fellowship was good. Know what I mean? It was like the blind date your roommate arranged for you in college. You asked, "What does she look like?

And he says, "She's got a great personality." Well—it was one of those hunts.

Anyway, back to the "wet-can-be-mighty-disagreeable" part. As we were wading toward land, I noticed that my friend was taking an apparently unnecessary and circuitous route to the intended terminus of our water fowl expedition. In other words, we were going a long way to cover a short distance, and with my short legs, this was getting old fast.

Without bothering to ask if there was some rhyme or reason for his meanderings, I headed straight for shore. After a couple of yards, just as I reached his peripheral vision, I remember hearing Olin say, "Watch out for the . . ."

When I resurfaced, blowing COLD Pearl River water like a baby whale, I heard the conclusion of his message, "..... ..les." I realized the "les" went with "stump holes!"

As we get into the harvest season each year, I hope and pray that neither our farmers nor our outdoorsmen will experience too much of the disagreeable results of being wet.

Having a beautiful, dry fall every year might be a long shot, but...

Whatever you do, don't be afraid to go with the long shots. Live life to its fullest every moment and be ready!

"And I said, 'Oh, that I had wings like a dove! For then I would fly away and be at rest.'"(Psalms 55:6)

GRAY GHOSTS

In case you haven't noticed, their numbers are growing dramatically. As the first weekend in September draws nearer, the influx will become noticeably greater. Who are they? Just go out in your backyard in the late afternoon and listen for a few minutes. You'll hear them. If you have one of those outdoor feeders, you'll see an increase in the number of the cooing mourning doves.

Dove season is almost upon us and once again preparations and reservations are being made at a feverish pace. Phone lines are beginning to sing, and the fields of milo and wheat are attracting more and more attention. Hunters can be seen making preparations for "Opening Day," and they're not alone. The doves are making preparations and reservations as well.

To the casual observer, all this excitement and enthusiastic activity probably seems a bit strange. While hunters are busy preparing to go out to the neighboring fields, the doves are busy moving their families and belongings to town where the danger is limited to a few bad youngsters with BB guns and a manageable number of house cats.

The opening of another dove season is at least as significant to the hunters as New Year's is to drunks! For those of us who love the thrill of the darting and diving demons of the sky, the night before Opening Day is just like New Year's Eve.

Over a month before the season opened one fall, I was talking to a Deacon in the Presbyterian Church at Mize. The conversation, which began over concern for a death in the church family, soon turned to the coming event. James Hugh Lack just happened to get off on the subject and mention that the milo field was looking mighty fine that year. The number of doves was up and opening day held real promise for the first time in several years.

"If you can swing it, you oughta come on down and join us for THE hunt." Sounded good to me!

Whether it's a novice hunter's very first hunting season or a "seasoned" veteran's umpteenth, the dawning of dove season is filled with as much excitement as a bridegroom waiting for his wedding. Sleep is usually non-existent the night before. Visions of missed shots interrupt a fitful sleep. The hunter sits straight up in the bed at one in the morning, convinced he heard laughter coming from somewhere in the darkness.

Every opening day is a thrill, filled with stories which have been told over and over again, as well as those waiting to be told for the very first time. Those who gather for the inauguration of each new dove season are linked together by a tight bond that neither miles nor months apart can tarnish or sever. Opening day of dove season is like a family reunion, except there won't be any cousins you'd rather not see!

Those who are opposed to hunting will rue the slaughter of all those doves on the first day of the season, but they don't realize that 80% of the annual dove hatch will die one way or the other. If just a few of the anti's would go out to an opening day shindig, they'd realize that we hunters aren't the blood thirsty killers they imagine.

When we get through laughing and visiting and go out to hunt, we've already scared half the dove population into town for the anti-hunters to enjoy. When we take to the field with our trusty shotguns, we train what's left in the art of maneuvering and scheduling. If you don't believe me, just watch the doves a few days into the season. Even when they fly over the peaceful streets, they'll be dipping, diving, and practicing their stalls and high speed climbs. You'll notice that they've changed their feeding schedules to ensure that they're all lined up on your powerlines during the hours when us hunters are most likely to be out hunting.

Enjoying the coming of another hunting season may be a long shot for you, but...

Whatever you do, don't be afraid to go with the long shots. Live life to its fullest every moment and be ready!

"So he(Noah) waited yet another seven days and sent out the dove, which did not return again to him anymore." (Genesis 8:12)

DELICIOUS DOVES

Although yours truly has had many an excellent dove hunt on opening Saturday, the great success that most folks enjoy in the Delta's dove fields after opening day is a matter of rumor, hearsay, and assumption. I've visited numerous fields subsequent to opening day, and the evidence often indicates high levels of success.

Opening day of the 1993 season was one of the best ever because of friends who invited me to their hunt. Some of our local Boy Scouts got together and prepared a field (legally mind you) for the hunt. They went out numerous mornings and afternoons in an attempt to gauge the numbers of birds using the field and determine the best possible spot to have a good hunt. Then these young men called their Scoutmaster and invited him (me) to come and take the best spot! With young people of this character, it sounds like there's hope for the future, don't ya think?.

By the end of the Labor Day weekend the Wimans had enough doves for supper a couple of times. The first was a delicious meal of fried doves, rice and gravy, biscuits, and green beans. Yum ... When the meal was over, nary a bird was left, but the best was yet to come.

One evening during the following week, having filleted the doves, we applied lemon pepper, garlic powder, a little worcestershire sauce and margarine and cooked shish-ka-bobs on the grill. Folded in the arms of onions, mushrooms, bellpeppers, and squash, the doves were so tender and delicious that it was a pure shame. I never before saw my wife growl at the children just for wanting another couple of filleted doves! Tsk, tsk, tsk.

A lot of dove hunters I know think that the dark meat of the bird is pretty yucky, not to be mentioned in the same month as the qualitatively superior quail. These folks just haven't tried the above-mentioned recipe. They're probably like my older brother.

The Thomas Milton "Sonny" Wiman recipe for doves consists of the following instructions:

139

Mix salt and pepper with flour and dust the dove breasts. Fry 'em up in an iron skillet, make gravy from the leavin's, and bake a dozen or so golden brown cathead biscuits.

Pour the gravy over the biscuits and a big old bed of hot, steaming rice, then dump the doves in the trash.

Readers following this tried and tested recipe for doves, however, are missing a mighty fine treat. With so many different ways to fix doves and really enjoy them, it's a shame to miss out on all the fun. Folks who think that the enjoyment is over when the dove folds and falls are badly mistaken. The cleaning part isn't fun, but after preparing a meal of fresh doves, watching your family head-down in the feed trough is a blast!

If you need help with recipes for cooking doves, check out Billy Joe Cross' *Cooking Wild Game and Fish* or *Outdoor Tables and Tales*. The latter is a product of the Southeaster Outdoor Press Association and would make a great gift for the hunter or hunter's wife at any time of the year.

Even if you're not a hunter, you can enjoy the fruits of other people's labors. Just ask a neighbor or family member who hunts to bring you a few doves and give them a try. In a way, though, I hope you don't like dove too much, because you'll probably take my spot in the dove field next September!

Enjoying a good dove hunt and meal may be a long shot for you, but...

Whatever you do, don't be afraid to go with the long shots. Live life to its fullest every moment and be ready!

"No other trees by the waters are ever to tower proudly on high, lifting their tops above the thick foliage."(Ezekiel 31:14)

CRUISIN'

The warm waters of Wolf Lake, a long, narrow, winding ox-bow, sparkled like millions of diamonds. Here and there fish jumped, momentarily stealing a few precious gems from the ocean of rippling jewels. Heat waves shimmered across the surface of the quiet lake hovering like blankets of air. It was a perfect day for cruisin'.

A large red buoy, which once graced the wide girth of the mighty Mississippi River, to guide tows on their incessant journeys from Memphis to New Orleans, stood guard at the dock. Speeding ski boats and wild-eyed children on jet skis are waved off by the bouncing buoy, protecting people and boats from unwanted incursions and possible collisions.

As we cruised, with the pontoons slicing through the remarkably clear water, I noted the bald cypress trees lining the lake. These giant trees mark the boundaries of many of our delta lakes for miles and miles. Spanish moss lends a stately appearance to the tall cypress, looking like bearded, Southern gentlemen.

Along the calm, muddy edges of the lake, cypress knees rise up and dot the shallows like dozens of wooden stalagmites. As the lake widens, the cypresses thin. Those which grow tall enough look down on their leafy cousins, obviously proud of their stature, even though they've been denuded of their tops by the lightning blows of God. Boney fingers of once luxuriant foliage point here and there as if to say, "HE did it!"

An occasional dove, kingfisher, and red-winged black bird drift lazily across from one shore to the other, perhaps searching for a shady spot. A frightened cormorant donates a feather for one cruisin' guest to sport in his mesh cap.

Late in the day, owls start their daily discussion about the approaching dusk. Wood ducks come barrelling down the edge of the lake, diving headlong into the tiny opening of their cypress chalets. No matter how many times I watch the beautifully plumed blurs plunge into their dens, I'm amazed that they can negotiate the diminutive entrance and stop quickly enough to avoid serious injury or death.

Lake houses, old rusty trailers, and a small camper dot the shore, reminding me that man makes his mark on even the most serene settings. Bobbing beer cans likewise testify to our stupidity and lack of concern for God's glorious creation.

All in all, cruisin' down a peaceful lake on a hot summer Saturday is mighty relaxing. Because of the fast-paced, stress-filled lives we tend to lead today, a few hours on the lake, easing along on a nice, perfectly equipped party boat, kicking back with friends, is mighty close to heaven.

Getting out and cruisin' down the lake with friends might be a long shot for you, but...

Whatever you do, don't be afraid to go with the long shots. Live life to its fullest every moment and be ready!

"Likewise you husbands, dwell with them with understanding, giving honor to the wife, as to the the weaker vessel, and as being heirs together of the grace of life, that your prayers may not be hindered."(I Peter 3:7)

HUNTIN' WIVES

Huntin' wives — wives of men who hunt — huntin' widows — are some of the expressions used to describe the women whose husbands suffer from a disease as ordinary as the common cold. This disease strikes in one form or another throughout the year, it's nearest kin being football in the fall, fishing in the spring, and golf in the summer. When winter approaches, women beware!

Years ago, when I was courting Miss Dorothy, I let her in on the fact that I suffer from the deep dark disease known as Hunticus Bodacious. At first, she didn't grasp the seriousness of my condition, but it wasn't long before she began to catch on to some of the symptoms and side effects which tend to affect those closest to the sufferers.

In an attempt to break her in gently, the first date I took her on was to a football game. By observing my intense interest and involvement in this first cousin to my illness, I knew she would get a glimpse of what she was getting herself into.

Not long thereafter, having survived the first brush with my sport's symptoms, we were to go out to eat one evening. About thirty minutes before I was to pick her up, I called from a pay phone at a country store about as far back in the boonies in Rankin County as I could get without needing a passport to get back to civilization.

"Sorry, Dorothy, but I'm gonna be late."

"How late?"

"Well, Olin and I got stuck trying to get out of the muddy field where we were working on our duck blind."

"Are you on your way now?"

"Well, we're still waiting on a friend of ours to bring his tractor over to pull us out."

"What time do you think you'll pick me up?"

"What time is it now?"

"Six-thirty."

"How about nine?"

"NINE?"

As you can imagine, our date that evening was impacted rather significantly by this unexpected muddy malady. Being late for important dates is only one of the side effects of the disease.

At times, the contagion manifests itself in other forms. Sometimes it crops up in terms of hunting nomenclature. Sometimes wives really struggle with the technical terminology which we hunters employ. The resulting misunderstandings can take on symptoms which range from deathly serious to hilariously humorous.

Not being one of those tattletales who lets the world in on the family secrets, I'll hold it down to a few of the hilariously humorous episodes.

One of my earliest and best hunting buddies was Olin Thomas. The brother of an ex-girlfriend, Olin was a special guy in his own right. It has taken years for Dorothy to understand the bond that Olin and I shared, which had nothing whatsoever to do with his sister. When the hunting virus is involved, no other plague, such as old girlfriends should even be considered. Hunting wives really struggle with some of the symptoms, don't you see?

Back to the nomenclature part of the pestilence. Olin saw Dorothy and me in Brandon one day and stopped to tell us about his newest and most promising therapeutic answer to the strain of our common contagion known as Duckitis.

The aggravation of having to climb out of a comfortable blind in order to chase dead and dying ducks all around Ross Barnett Reservoir had demonstrated the need for a good retriever. We had tried numerous breeds without much success.

There was the banker's son we took on one occasion. He was too soft for the job. Then there was the teacher's son. He was too intelligent to fall for our tricks. We even tried an athlete, but he proved to be too much to handle. He managed to throw both of us out of the blind almost simultaneously when we suggested for the tenth time that, since he was nearest the door, he pick up the duck that was floating off.

Olin finally ran up on the correct diagnosis. "I've got a

black lab," he beamed as he got out of his tan-colored Volkswagen Thing.

Dorothy didn't say anything at the moment, but when we got home, she said, "When did Olin start fooling around with a black lab?" Not being familiar with this abbreviated terminology for a black labrador retriever, a dog, nor being close enough to Olin to know of his sterling character, she had a picture in her mind of a secret dope lab in which Olin was employing black light to grow his weeds.

Hunters, take note. When you tell your girlfriend or wife, "Hon, I'm gonna take my .270 with 150 grain boat tails, get in my 4X4, and take a stand on the edge of some cut-over to wait for a Boone and Crockett ten-pointer to appear at the optimum time according to the Solunar Table," don't be too surprised if she begins to demonstrate some of the symptoms of that malevolent malady known as Hunticus Bodacious Wificus Cussyououticus.

Wives and girlfriends who honestly understand the disease we hunters suffer from may be a long shot, but...

Whatever you do, don't be afraid to go with the long shots. Live life to its fullest every moment and be ready!

"And so it was, in the morning that Jonathan went out into the field at the time appointed with David, and a little lad was with him. Then he said to his lad, `now run, find the arrows which I shoot.'"(1 Samuel 20:35-36)

STICK AND STRING SEASON

To those in tune with the changing seasons and the sudden rise in 4WD traffic on the streets and highways of the Mississippi Delta, the first of October each year signals the opening of deer season. As far as the hunters are concerned, it never arrives a day too soon.

Each fall, the Mississippi Department of Wildlife oversees the first round of deer season, which is always with the bow and arrow. Officially known as "Archery Season," each year's bow season is a smidgin different from past years. Change is the optimum word for regulations concerning the hunting of deer with stick and string here in Mississippi.

For example, during the first two weeks of the '93 season, for the first time ever, the bow hunter was limited to forked-horn bucks only. Neither spike bucks nor does could be taken during this period. This wise move enabled does to wean their fawns and thus prevented the loss of doe and fawn, which happened no tellng how many times in the past. After the first two weeks, the bow hunter was then allowed to legally take two does and five bucks during the rest of the bow season. The liberal limit of deer for gun hunters remained five bucks and three does.

Another tell-tale sign that the deer season is upon us each fall comes through the air waves, the wonders of modern communication. In the past, we've turned our television dial to TNN on Saturdays at 11:00(Central) and have seen the very fine "North American Sportsman" with Gary Morris. We've seen tarpon landed on fly rods in the Florida Keys and a black bear hunt with a long bow in Alaska. One of the episodes that I especially enjoyed was a thrilling buffalo hunt on horseback with the Oglala Sioux Indians using flat bows!

Besides the fine "North American Sportsman" on Saturdays, TNN also broadcasts "Buckmasters Whitetail Magazine" with Jackie Bushman at 12:30 on Sunday afternoon. This top notch production keeps yours truly from preaching too long! The Buckmasters Top Bow Indoor World Championships are always mighty impressive. You wouldn't have believed your eyes when Jackie Caudle of Gadsden, Alabama, broke the tie and won this outstanding competition in 1993. Those guys can shoot a bow!

Now then, if all this talk about these super hunting and fishing shows doesn't get you out of that chair and into the woods, let me share one more sign that the time has come to get out and enjoy what the Good Lord has given us.

Author of some 15 outdoor books, John Phillips is an author who will get us out of the house and into the woods. *The Masters' Secrets of Bowhunting Deer* is a truly outstanding piece of outdoor literature. No bowhunter should miss the opportunity to purchase a copy of this book and read it as soon as possible. You'll benefit immediately from the down-to-earth, practical information you'll gain from its pages. John has interviewed some of the nation's best bowhunters and gleaned what you and I need to be more successful bowhunters. Even the latest trends in bowhunting are included in this book. What's that? Would you believe that bowhunting is the fastest growing sport among...women? Look out men. Your wife may want a compound bow for Christmas! John may be right about this trend, but you'll know that the trend has arrived when you see the ambulance backed up to the door at 503 Holmes St. That's when I'll be having a coronary over Dorothy asking me to take her hunting!(to order this fine book, send $11.95 check or money order to Night Hawk Publications, P.O. Drawer 375, Fairfield, AL 35064 or call 1-800-627-4295 for VISA or MasterCard orders-mention you heard about it in *Long Shots* and John promises to autograph and date it for you)

If all the activity, TV shows, and great new books don't get you headed for the woods, maybe you ought to stop by our house and check out the pair of eight-pointers. Such can be the results of following the sage advice of the experts.

If getting you excited about deer hunting is a long shot, then I truly hope that whatever you do, you won't be afraid to go with the long shots. Live life to its fullest every moment and be ready!

"Then the Lord opened the mouth of the donkey, and she said to Balaam, `What have I done to you, that you have struck me these three times?' And Balaam said to the donkey, `Because you have abused me. I wish there were a sword in my hand, for now I would kill you!' So the donkey said to Balaam, `Am I not your donkey on which you have ridden, ever since I became yours, to this day? Was I ever disposed to do this to you?' And he said,`No.'" (Numbers 22:28-30)

ADVICE TO A YOUNG SQUIRREL

I overheard a conversation the other day that you might be interested in. There was this soon-to-be mamma squirrel talking to her mother about the ways of the world.

"To begin with," she began, "forget living outside of the city limits."

"Why's that, Mamma?" the rookie limb rat queried.

"Human beings stalk through your neighborhood from September through January when you live out in the country," she explained.

"But aren't there dangers in the city too?" the rookie continued, questioning the wisdom of her elder (sounds familiar, doesn't it, parents?).

"Yes, there are cats and dogs to contend with in the city. And yes, there are the cars and trucks you have to watch out for. Don't overlook the dangers of electric wires either."

The whole idea of moving inside the city limits and setting up house didn't sound so safe to this young high-rise rodent. In fact, it sounded down right dangerous to live in such proximity to human beings, seeing as how they're actually domesticated defectors from the animal kingdom.

"If you ask me, the whole thing sounds mighty dumb. What benefits could possibly outweigh the dangers?"

"Well, there's always the ban against hunting us inside the city limits. That's kinda nice, even though there are some really mean-spirited younguns that kill a cousin every now and then with a BB gun or a pellet rifle. Most of the younger humans are pretty nice though. They think we're kinda cute and nice to have around."

The novice nut-cracker, not wanting to appear too disrespectful mentioned almost under her breath, "I guess BB's or pellets aren't so bad, unless, of course, it's your hide they cut to pieces with the things."

"Yes, dear, that is a danger, but as long as you keep a keen eye out for cats and little boys with BB guns, you'll be just fine. Most folks make sure that we have plenty to eat, even if the acorn and pecan crop is short. Some nice people even put up what they call "bird feeders," which are really there to challenge us to put on a show for them. They like to see all the innovative ways we get around their obstacles."

"All sounds kinda tough to me, though."

"Life is tough, kid, and you better learn that lesson early on. I've found that this town is about the nicest place in the world to live and raise a family. I've even heard most of the people saying the same thing, so it must be true."

The younger bushy tail conceded, "Well, I guess I'll give it a try then. Is there anything else that I need to know?"

"Yes, dear, there's lots, but one last warning will do for now."

"Yeah, what's that?"

"Whatever you do, if you run across a chinaberry tree, don't eat the berries."

"Why's that?"

"The last time I sat around in a chinaberry tree eating those delicious delights, I got drunk as a skunk (I guess that's where the term "stinking drunk" comes from) and fell out of the tree on the way home. Honey, it just doesn't pay to eat and run!"

As you well know, animals have spoken on other occasions. The serpent of old spoke to Adam and Eve, but it was a rotten conversation. Many times, our little dog, Fuzzy, has a word or two for us. But, you're no doubt thinking that I'm pulling your leg with all this talk about a conversation between two squirrels. So what if I am?

Talking squirrels may be a long shot for you, but... Whatever you do, don't be afraid to go with the long shots. Live life to its fullest every moment and be ready!

"The clouds poured out water; The skies sent out a sound; Your arrows also flashed about." (Psalms 77:17)

TO BE OR NOCK TO BE

Shakespeare's Hamlet first made the comment, "To be or not to be, that is the question. Whether 'tis nobler in the mind to suffer the slings and arrows of outrageous for-tune, or die...that is the question." On a recent bow hunting trip, I ran into a modern version of that famous quote— "To be or nock to be, that is the frustration."

The age of sophisticated technology has affected every area of life, and hunting is no exception. In the old days, the only bows available for the archer who wanted to hunt big game were long bows. Outside of Merry Old England, there weren't many Robin Hoods who could hit anything at all with such a weapon.

Good old Yankee know-how brought in the age of the recurve, which enabled less than expert bow and arrow enthusiasts to get into the game(in a manner of speaking).

After a few years of trying to bag a big game animal with the recurves, folks like Fred Bear and others decided that the only way to encourage the masses to bow hunt would be to come up with an easier weapon to use. Abra kadabra: the compound bow.

With these combinations of cables, wheels, cams, stabiliz-ers, sights, silencers, overdraws, cellular phones, range finders, and portable blinds, even a novice could go to the woods and hunt with a bow and arrow. With the wide range in prices, just about anybody could afford to bow hunt. (Bows without cellular phones are a bit cheaper!)

No matter how sophisticated, technologically advanced, or affordably priced, no bow will do the job unless the hopeful hunter practices. When I first started bow hunting, I practiced nearly year round. As I grow older, and after numerous successful hunts with my inexpensively priced bow, I've begun to practice less and less.

Prior to the opening day of bow season for whitetail deer a few years ago, I finally realized that with season about to open, I needed to shoot a few arrows. Being the sharpshooter that I am, most hit their mark. Well, they were close enough for horseshoes and hand grenades.

Truth is, I paid very little attention to anything except the foam-filled deer target. I didn't put up any red dots to concentrate on, and as it turned out, this was a fatal flaw in my preparations.

Opening day arrived, and I drove out to the hills and scouted around for a good place to put up my ladder stand. Easing through a small patch of cut-over timber, I jumped four deer in the space of a few hundred yards. Plenty of other sign was evident, so I put my stand against a nice oak tree and prepared for the afternoon hunt.

A slight breeze was blowing out of the northeast with a breath of freshness in its gentle caress. The sun was sliding lazily toward the horizon, its rays of warmth withdrawing steadily toward the west when I decided to try one of my deer calls. It was one made by a new friend, Mr. Eli Haydel, owner of Haydel Game Calls of Bossier City, Louisiana.

Several soft grunts brought the nice doe bounding out of her cover to within twelve steps of my tree stand. My nerves couldn't have been more active if she had been a huge he-deer. The doe presented a perfect broadside shot as I nervously nocked my arrow, pulled back to full draw, aimed just behind her front shoulder, and . . .

"Good grief! Why is my broadhead pointing down at my arrow rest?"

With one eye on the deer, one eye on the strangely positioned arrow, and one eye on the nock (the place on the bow string where the end of the arrow shaft is placed/the extra eye was my nervous condition) . . . You can see my dilemma, can't you?

153

Since I don't have three eyes, I was in a quandry trying to figure out the problem.

Shaking from fatigue and mounting frustration, I released the arrow, sending it spiraling toward its intended target. The camouflaged shaft immediately assumed a steep angle of descent, its flight path causing it to strike the earth nowhere near the doe. As I nocked my second arrow, I realized what I had done. Because of my lack of practice, I had nocked my arrow on top of the mark on the bow string(the nock), instead of below it. I really "belowed" that shot, didn't I?

"To be, or nock to be, that was the question." The question of whether it was nobler in the mind to sling an arrow successfully or not was answered in short order. Clearly, this was "nock" to be the day of the hunter. In fact, I had to let the deer stagger (she could hardly maintain her balance while holding her flanks with both front legs, bent over in agony from all the laughter) away as I stood there laughing at myself. When the doe stopped to snort a few yards away, I believe I detected a wheeze. Could it have been asthma?

For all you bow hunters out there who have already been successful, congratulations! For those who have gone and missed, let me reassure you. You're not alone!

Putting delicious venison on your table with a bow and arrow, a stick and a string, may be a long shot, but...

Whatever you do, don't be afraid to go with the long shots. Live life to its fullest every moment and be ready!

"Now a wind went out from the Lord, and it brought quail from the sea and left them fluttering near the camp..."

(Numbers 11:31a)

MR. BOB WHITE

Some, will no doubt rememer when quail were plentiful in the Delta. Today, about the only place to hear "Bob White" is in an orthodontist'soffice in Greenwood(Dr. Robert White).

What happened? It depends on whom you ask. Some say DDT is the culprit. Others claim farming edge to edge, leaving little or no cover caused the loss. Still others blame the demise of quail on fire ants, coyotes, fox, or game hogs.

The best answer doesn't solve the problem. It's just a shame that the days of the gentleman's sport of quail hunting are all but gone. Why, I can remember when quail were as thick as fleas on a walker dog in the heat of summer, and you never knew what you might come home with after a long day afield.

When I was pastor of the small Calvary Presbyterian Church in rural Smith County, an octogenarian shared the following account of an amazing quail hunt. Seems that the two best wing shots of the era were trying out a new dog, but the setter wouldn't work for them.

A call to the owner summoned him to their hunting spot, the dog began to work the way their $1,000 said he was supposed to. No sooner had they turned him out of the truck than he pointed again and again. The covey got up and both expert marksmen fired two shots apiece. The dog retrieved three birds and then disappeared over a little hill.

When the dog didn't return with the fourth bird, one of the

men said, "I ain't never seen you miss, Brother Jim!"

"Me? It must've been you that done the missin'!"

Before the conversation turned into a full blown discussion, the dog owner said, "Let's go look for the dog. He's probably found a cripple or a single."

Over the rise and down into a creek bottom, the hunters trudged, the two shooters still arguing over who missed. "There's ole Joe, and he's pointed there on the edge of the crik."

They eased up to the edge of the creek but could see nothing. The water was some 8-10 feet below the edge. "There ain't no bird here. The dog's lying."

"He ain't never lied afore. Go ahead, Joe!"

The dog leaped off the bank and plunged into the water below. A terrible struggle ensued. It looked like Tarzan wrestling with an alligator in one of those old movies. Then Joe emerged from the depths and climbed back up the bank. In his mouth was a large bass.

"Well, I never!" they all chimed in at once. The dog's former owner took the bass from Joe and opened its mouth, and guess what? There was the fourth quail!

Some die-hards still tell tall tales about Mr. Bob White and pursue the thundering, feathery rockets in the hills on private land or on game preserves with pen-raised birds. With two Brittany spaniels on the payroll, the preserves have become an annual ritual for this die-hard. Two or three times yearly Jack and Brutus make all the expense of keeping them up well worth it.

One frosty, February afternoon, a good friend and I had two dozen quail set out on a rolling pasture in Grenada County. With Sure Shot Game Preserve's best on the loose, we commenced the hunt.

Jack, the older and more experienced of the two dogs, locked up like a statue on a pair of birds. Each hunter was given a clean shot on the rise, and both dogs had a bird each to retrieve, which they dutifully accomplished to the delight of their owner.

A third bird suddenly shot up wild and was crippled by a long shot. Jack pointed the wounded bird in a briar patch about two hundred yards away.

The bird couldn't fly, and wouldn't budge. The dog refused to break his point on a live bird, thus presenting a dilemma. After I suffered through several painful encounters with previously unused thorns, the bird was in the bag.

I looked around for the dog who was obviously too intelligent to crawl into the briar patch. He was sitting on the tailgate of the pick-up, drinking a caffeine-free Coke and smoking a Picayune cigarette.

Well, the days of quail hunting as a gentleman's sport may be nearly dead, but the tales associated with it are still tall and the shots are still long, so...

Whatever you do, don't be afraid to go with the long shots. Live life to its fullest every moment and be ready!

"The heavens declare the glory of God; and the firmament shows His handiwork. Day unto day utters speech, and night unto night reveals knowledge. There is no speech or language where their voice is not heard. Their line is gone out though all the earth, and their words to the end of the world. In them He has set a tabernacle for the sun, which is like a bridegroom coming out of his chamber, and rejoices like a strong man to run its race. Its rising is from one end of heaven, and its circuit to the other end; and there is nothing hidden from its heat."(Psalms 19:1-6)

SUNSETS

One of my favorite times of day is sunset. Though a mere child of forty-something, I've seen some mighty fine sunsets over the years.

Back in 1974-75, Dorothy and I served as missionaries on the island of Grenada, a tiny dot of land in the Lesser Antilles. This beautiful tropical island is home to some 100,000 people, and our task was to help start a church in the capitol city of St. Georges.

While we were living in St. Georges, we were privileged to witness some breathtaking sunsets from the veranda of our rented home. For a short period of time while we were there, a volcano was erupting in Nicaragua. The resulting volcanic clouds sprayed high into the sky to our west and provided amazing sunsets for us. We watched in awe as, day after day, the deep red and brilliant orange of the volcanic ash enveloped the golden orb of sun as it rushed toward the horizon, that imaginary line where the blue of the tropical sky and the green of the Caribbean caress each other.

Those awesome sunsets marked the passage of day after day for us newlyweds so far from home for the first time in our lives. Though some signs of passage in life are painful, others are like welcome friends. Sunsets like those on the island of Grenada are truly a blessing.

At the time, I thought I'd never see a sunset as glorious as those in the West Indies. I was wrong. Our sunsets here in the Mississippi Delta, signs of the passage of yet another day in our lives, can be as glorious as anywhere in the world.

I can't imagine a prettier sight than that of a westward

158

glance in September and October in the Delta. If you haven't taken a late afternoon ride during cotton picking time, you should make plans to come see us during the harvest season. You'll see sunsets like you've never seen before.

The sight of cottonpickers scurrying back and forth, pulling cotton, like taffy from the stalks and dumping the cuddly loads into trailers or module builders is fascinating. The dust they stir up racing back and forth down the turnrows creates a filter through which to view truly glorious sunsets.

For a short time, the colors surrounding the descending sun change constantly, providing a natural panorama of breathtaking beauty.

Sunsets can also be totally awesome from inside the sanctuary of our Presbyterian Church here in Belzoni. The stained-glass window in the western end of the building is situated directly behind the pulpit. When the sun nears the end of its circuit for the day, the window seems to come to life. The rays of light diffuse through the various panels of different colors and create a sight that is very close to divine. The aura is one that your imagination can quickly associate with the resurrection of Christ in the light of that first Easter sunrise or the glowing presence of Christ on the mount of transfiguration.

Whether they're viewed from an island in the West Indies, a Delta cottonfield, or through the stained-glass windows of a stately church, sunsets are awe-inspiring signs of passage. They mark the end of day and the beginning of night.

Signs of passage such as sunsets are all around us. All of us have signs of passage that we look forward to with anticipation. Whether it's opening day of deer season, the first college football game of a new season, time to plant a crop in the spring or harvest it in the fall, we all observe the signs of passage in this life with varying degrees of excitement.

Some of the signs of passage aren't as appealing as others. The final football game, the last day of deer season, the last day of a family vacation, or the final illness of a loved one or friend are real down times for us. These signs of passage don't affect us in the same way as a glorious sunset.

159

When it comes to the signs of passage marking the end of our days here on earth, we get discouraged. But wait a minute! Just like the setting sun marks not just the end of the day but the beginning of a beautiful evening, so the final sign of passage in life can mark both an end and a beginning.

For those who trust in Jesus Christ as their Lord and Savior, the final sign of passage doesn't just mark the end of our earthly existence. It also marks the beginning of eternal life with God in heaven. It marks the beginning of real life, life like we've never experienced it before — glorious, unending.

When we breathe our last breath here on earth, we'll take the next breath in heaven, a breath of joy, happiness and peace, no pain, no sorrow, no tears, no death, the end of the signs of passage.

You're probably thinking, "Boy, this is sure different from the other chapters I've read. Well, I guess it is, but then I believe that, from time to time, we all need to pause and take stock of where we've been, what's going on around us, and where we're headed.

A glorious Delta sunset in the fall of the year is a perfect time for such reflection. That golden day's end is a sign of passage, a reminder that we are all just passing through this world.

Reflecting on the direction your life is taking may be a long shot for you, but...

Whatever you do, don't be afraid to go with the long shots. Live life to its fullest every moment and be ready!

"He also prepares for Himself instruments of death; He makes His arrows into fiery shafts." (Psalms 7:13)

STRAIGHT AS AN ARROW

Have you ever wondered where we got the old saying, "Straight as an arrow?" I sure have. Maybe it was Robin Hood or Little John speaking in reference to Robin, "He's straight as an arrow." Perhaps it was the Indians of North America who prompted the Pale Face to start using the expression, "They're straight as an arrow."

No matter what its origin, the phrase has very picturesque and graphic meaning. Only the straight arrow flies correctly and accurately. If an arrow isn't straight, it isn't worth a hoot nor a holler. Well, it's probably worth a holler, because the archer who shoots an arrow that isn't straight will certainly be doing plenty of hollering before he's done.

On my den wall, I have a plaque with a set of small buck horns and hoofs from the first deer I took with a bow. The story unfolded like an accordion years ago down in Smith County.

A friend and neighbor across the creek had bought a compound bow and suggested I give it a try. In an attempt to cover what I was sure to be total embarrassment, I said, "No thanks, Houston, I probably couldn't hit a bull in the behind with a bass fiddle." After watching him shoot at an old oil can a couple of times, I decided I couldn't do any worse than he was doing and gave it a try.

To the demise of our bank account that month, I hit the oil can on the second or third attempt. Before the week was out, I was practicing with a new bow and a half dozen new arrows.

My first attempt at deer hunting came sooner than I expected, and the results were predictable. After shooting all my arrows at a spike buck never more than 20 yards from my tree stand, I unsheathed my hunting knife and tossed it at him too! Apparently my arrows weren't straight, don't you see?

Having checked the shafts for their straightness and discovering that they were indeed straight as an arrow, I decided that practice was the order of the days that followed.

After a couple of weeks, I was once again invited to go bow hunting. This time, I sat for hours on end (and a sore one at that!) waiting for a deer to appear. From 5 a.m. until 10:40 a.m., nothing showed up. Suddenly, there was a terrible commotion to the west of my stand.

Without any thought of my sudden movement and the possibility that it might frighten the deer off, I rose to my feet and watched in amazement as a buck came tearing through the woods at breakneck speed. He ran straight as an arrow to my stand and plowed the ground to a stop some ten yards away.

As he came to a stop, broadside to me, I released the arrow. WHOP! A perfect shot — but the deer turned and began to walk calmly away. Violent shivers suddenly came on me without warning. A casual observer would have concluded that I was suffering from a high fever or a case of the DT's. Bewildered and disturbed, I watched in disbelief as the deer paused for a minute to nibble at something on his flank, then resume his leisurely retreat.

Just as I remembered that I had more arrows in the quiver, he stopped, shuddered, and fell in his tracks. Tenderloin for supper! The feathery missile had flown as straight as an arrow to the desired target. A perfect shot had done quick work.

After climbing down from the tree stand, I found my arrow on the ground where the deer had paused to nibble at his flank. He had pulled the arrow out! Ever since, I have kept the arrows that have brought home meat on the feet of that first deer taken with the bow. The bent and broken arrows are a constant reminder that I must shoot straight as an arrow if I want to bring home some delicious venison for the table.

Whether you bow hunt or not, I hope that you shoot straight as an arrow with your fellow man. Even if it IS a long shot for you, we would all be so much better off if everyone would live according to this ancient maxim, "Straight as an arrow."

So...

Whatever you do, don't be afraid to go with the long shots.
Live life to its fullest every moment and be ready!

"A friend loves at all times, and a brother is born for adversity."
(Proverbs 17:17)

A FINE AND PHEASANT MEMORY

Garth Brooks be-
came a household fixture
by singing about his friends
in low places down at the
Oasis. Well, if it counts for
anything with anybody, I
have some special friends who took me to Al's Oasis.

To get to Al's Oasis from the Mississippi Delta, take
Highway 55 north to Memphis, board a Delta flight to either Rapid
City or Sioux Falls, then rent a vehicle and drive on down
Highway 90 to Chamberlain, South Dakota. You can't miss THE
hot spot of this sleepy little farming community.

Several times a year, the quiet community becomes a
thriving, booming, pulsing centrifuge of outdoor activity. When
the Walleye start running, fishermen from all over the world come
to Chamberlain. Talk about getting hooked! These folks have it
bad.

Seems as though every native becomes a guide, and there's
a fishing rig in every parking spot at the Hillside Motel. Even the
marquee in front of the churches have some comment designed to
lure fishermen into their worship service.

The second time each year the town goes through a
metamorphosis is early October. That's when pheasant season
opens.

Everywhere you look, there's a truck with a dog box or a
crowd of hunters standing in the parking lot of the motel admiring
each other's choice of the perfect shotgun for Opening Day.

In my case, some good friends treated me to a Chamberlain
pheasant hunt one fine October. We flew into Rapid City, which
is on the western side of South Dakota. A rented 4X4 Suburban
provided the transportation as we drove east through the Badlands.
What an awesome sight!

Arriving in Chamberlain, we passed Al's Oasis, which was

164

handily snuggled up against the Interstate. After a brief comment or two about the real magnetism of Al's Oasis, we headed across the wide Missouri River, which isn't all that wide at Chamberlain. The few, short, but tantalizing comments about Al's Oasis set my mouth to watering and mind to whirling.

The first morning, we re-crossed the Missouri River in darkness and headed to an Indian Reservation for a goose hunt. It was thrilling to see thousands upon thousands of Canada geese rising from the calm waters of the river, heading for the wheat fields just beyond our pit blinds.

Only one goose fell to the expert marksmanship of me and two other hunters, but we had a wonderful time. The snide comments about one another's aim and the depth of the blind (about eight feet!) caused the morning to pass all too quickly.

Noon came and it was time for the pheasant hunt to begin. Some 15-20 of us hunters, mostly Mississippi Delta boys, had gathered on a beautiful corn farm to the southeast of Chamberlain.

Within an hour, everyone in our party had a limit of the brightly colored pheasants. Few sights in this world are more beautiful than a cock pheasant thundering from cover just ahead of an advancing hunter.

"Nothing can beat this," I thought to myself. "A Canada goose in the morning and a limit of pheasant in the afternoon. Incredible! It can't get any better than this," or so I reckoned.

Then we went to Al's Oasis. A large dining area to the right awaited us as we entered the swinging doors. A spacious, tempting, shopping section beckoned off to the left. Like so many of the old-time hardware stores, Al's had everything you needed, plus a whole lot that you wanted just because it was there.

After great meals of prime rib the first night and walleye the next, I felt as though life was somehow fuller and richer than ever before (I sure was!).

The friends who took me and the new ones I made on the trip have made my life better. Folks, this is what hunting and fishing dreams are made of.

If you ever get the opportunity, don't pass up a fight with a Walleye or a shot at a thundering pheasant. While you're there, don't miss the Black Hills, Mount Rushmore, or the Badlands, which are among the natural attractions of this wonderful part of our country. And don't forget Al's Oasis either!

Even if a trip to South Dakota for the hunting or fishing trip of a lifetime is a long shot for you...

Whatever you do, don't be afraid to go with the long shots. Live life to its fullest every moment and be ready!

"O my soul, my soul! I am pained in my very heart! My heart makes a noise in me; I cannot hold my peace, because you have heard, O my soul, the sound of the trumpet, the alarm of war."

(Jeremiah 4:19)

TICK, TICK, TICK...

Alarm clocks. Who needs them? Well, I do for one. When it comes to waking up, I need all the help I can get. Even though I love mornings, if it weren't for alarm clocks, I'd miss most of them!

Alarm clocks have come in many shapes and sizes in my personal experience. Growing up in Brandon in the early 1950's, a traditional alarm clock wasn't required. Every morning, Monday through Friday, at exactly 6:30, I would hear my mother from the kitchen, "It's time to get up and get ready for school." Whether it was raining or sun shiny, whether I felt like a million bucks or sick as a mule, the mom-alarm went off with perfect timing and the exact same message.

Early on in my educational career, I tried to hit the snooze button of that alarm clock. "But Mom, my stomach hurts. I think I need to go back to bed and skip school today." In those days, paregoric and castor oil were the wonder drugs. A dose of one or the other and off I'd go — and go — and go — just like the Energizer Rabbit! After a few doses, I quit hitting the snooze button!

When I went off to college, my parents were concerned about me handling all that freedom. No more "It's time to get up and get ready for school", from my alarm clock of the past twelve years. So Mom bought me one of those wind-up jobs. On a scale of 1 to 10, that alarm was a 10 for its ability to wake the dead! The worst part of it, however, was that on a scale of 1 to 10, the thing made so much ticking noise that the living couldn't go to sleep.

My roommate complained so much about the tick-tick, tick-tick, tick-tick, that I tried hiding it. I put it under my pillow. It was like sleeping on the San Andreas fault during the 1989 San

Francisco earthquake! I hid it in my sock drawer. The wooden cabinet acted like a megaphone: TICK-TICK, TICK-TICK, TICK-TICK.

Finally one night, in desperation, though we were living on the third floor of the dormitory, I tossed the alarm clock out the window. The peace and quiet was deafening, so I went downstairs to see what was left. Much to our relief, the thing had landed in a shrub. I could hear it ticking as soon as I opened the door! Still today, I can wind that sucker up and it will "tick" me off.

When it comes to hunting, an alarm clock is absolutely essential. One evening I was preparing for the next day's deer hunt. Excited as a result of the scouting I had done and the sign I had found, I eagerly laid out all my clothes and equipment the night before. The last preparation was to set the alarm for 5:00 a.m.

The next morning, somewhere around 6:30, something went off inside my head. At first I thought it was light from the window. Wrong, at 5:00 in the morning, it's supposed to be dark. Then I thought it was Dorothy suddenly realizing I was supposed to have been gone by now. At last, the cobwebs cleared from my confused, sleepy, and now aggravated brain. It was the voice of my adolescent alarm clock, "It's 6:30 and time to get up and go to school." No doubt, my mother, though 90 miles away, thought I needed to go back to school to learn the difference between "AM" and "PM" on an alarm clock!

Waking up on time with or without the aid of an alarm clock may be a long shot for you, so...

Whatever you do, don't be afraid to go with the long shots. Live life to its fullest every moment and be ready!

"For what I am doing, I do not understand. For what I will to do, that I do not practice; but what I hate, that I do."

(Romans 7:15)

PARADOXES

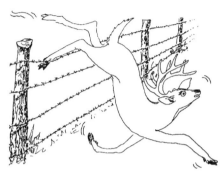

Know what a paradox is? Well, it isn't two exotic physicians, I can tell you that. According to Mr. Webster's way of thinking, a paradox is "a statement that seems contradictory, unbelievable, or absurd but that may actually be true in fact — something inconsistent with common experience or having contradictory qualities — a person who is inconsistent or contradictory in character or behavior."

In other words, most of our politicians are paradoxes, a malaise of opposites, saying one thing one day and the opposite the next. Since most politicians are also people just like you and me, it may be difficult to admit, but we are all paradoxes at times.

I ran square into the realization that I am sometimes a paradox when I was bowhunting one afternoon. It was a gorgeous day. The sun was shining brightly, with shafts of light like white streamers piercing through the leafy canopy of early fall. The temperature was just warm enough to anger the few remaining mosquitos. Buzzing around like the proverbial ag applicator (used to be aerial applicator, and before that, crop duster) defoliating the cotton crop, one pesky pest was relentless. After an application of Deerhunters Insect Repellent by Wisconsin Pharmacol, some of the best insect repellent I've ever used, that problem was solved. Not only is this stuff good as an insect repellent, the earth scent (smells like dirt), I believe, serves as a good masking scent to cover up natural human odors.

As the sun began to sink in the western sky, playful cat squirrels wrapped me up. An especially curious little fellow caught

169

sight of me from ten feet away in an adjacent tree and started a real ruckus. I whined softly back at him, and he was soon on his way to the top of the pin oak for a quick evening meal before sundown.

I had not seen or heard a deer until nearly dark. Suddenly, the woods erupted, the quiet of the dying day shattered by the fleeing four-footed fellow. A young buck, obviously leaving the scene of an early season joust with a more mature male, was high-tailing it for cover.

In a matter of minutes, it was too dark to see the sights on my compound bow. There were eight to ten deer all around my stand, but I couldn't see them!

A few more ticks of the clock, the first of the group was downwind of me and began to snort and tell all the others of human presence. At that point, I climbed down and walked out to my truck.

The headlights of the Toyota four wheel-drive pierced the darkness of the gravel road as I sped toward the main highway and home. Suddenly, out of nowhere, a nice 8-point buck jumped in front of the streaking truck.

Without hesitation, I slammed on the brakes and nearly lost control on the muddy road. The deer, nice and fat, acted as though nothing at all was wrong with the scene. He turned and started on down the middle of the road in front of me.

Going again, I followed the deer for nearly a hundred yards before he decided he didn't like all the light. Quickly he made a bound to the left, up a four-foot embankment, and over a barbed wire fence. Well, almost over the fence that is. He hung a back foot and turned a somersault.

Once again I stopped to enjoy the sight. Quite humorous actually, watching a nice, fat 8-point trying to regain his feet. Just like humans, he seemed to be looking around to see if anybody had seen him fall. Scrambling to his feet like a three-sheets-in-the-wind drunk, he headed off into the darkness.

At that moment, a thought hit me. Here I've been sitting in a tree for three hours trying to kill a deer with a sharp stick, and now a fine buck jumps right in my path. So what do I instinctively do? Nearly kill myself trying not to kill the deer! Talk about a paradox. There's one for you, for sure.

Understanding why hunters go out to kill but take a chance on killing themselves rather than killing one with a truck equipped with a huge bumper may be a long shot for you, but...

Whatever you do, don't be afraid to go with the long shots. Live life to its fullest every moment and be ready!

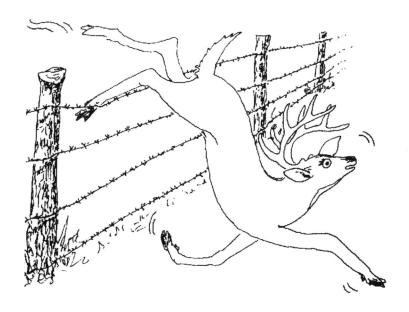

"In everything give thanks; for this is the will of God in Christ Jesus for you." (I Thessalonians 5:18)

THANKSGIVING

As the Lord gives me more and more opportunities to witness the annual celebration of Thanksgiving, I marvel at all that He has done for me and mine and our Country. Bear with me as I take you on a little outing of the mind.

Join me as we stroll along and consider what we have to be thankful for. Belzoni is like a lot of small towns across the Country. People of all ages and circumstances can be found up and down the streets and in various business establishments or in church on any Sunday morning.

With the changing of seasons and descent of autumn leaves, more than the limbs of stately oaks and brittle pecans are unmasked. We begin to see the heart and soul of a community.

The approach of the Thanksgiving and Christmas seasons tends to bring out the best in our little community. We see things that the leaves of spring and summer's activities and busy-ness conceal.

Walking down the peaceful streets, one is often the recipient of a friendly wave, the toot of a horn from a passing motorist accompanied by a tiny smirk or a big ole grin. The imitations of the ever present mockingbird, the sweet song of a cardinal courting his mate, or the chatter of bluejays playing chase with a squirrel are found on nearly every block.

In the evenings, a quiet walk after sunset yields the sound of gentle breezes, sending the remaining leaves cascading onto waiting lawns below. The few pines to be found around this peaceful little town yield a soft moan, the distant call of a horned owl down by the river proclaiming that someone still gives a "hoot." (Gotta have one pun, folks!)

We have so much to be thankful for. The muffled rays of corner street lights barely piercing the den drapes, yellow bug lights on carports, and numerous giant oaks breaking up our shadowy

172

stroll. In spite of the problems of any end-of-the-century town, this is a great place to live and raise a family.

By the time Thanksgiving arrives, businesses and streets are proclaiming the fast approach of the celebration of the Messiah's birth. A few more smiles can be had without much effort these days.

The season brings a sort of temporary revival. Even the orneriest merchants become God-fearing folks these days. I even overheard one merchant's family, who happens to be of another religious persuasion, gathered around the cash register, singing, "What a friend we have in Jesus!"

Seriously, we all have so much to be thankful for. Even amidst the pain and sorrow, the trials and tribulations of life, we have an abundance of reasons to give thanks.

As a group, hunters are often accused, and rightly so many times, of being pretty self-centered and narrowly-focused once deer season rolls around. I confess that I too often spend all or at least part of Thanksgiving Day at deer camp instead of with my family. Our earthly families and our heavenly one should command more importance in our lives than they sometimes do.

In reality, my greatest blessing on this earth besides knowing Jesus as my Lord and Savior is having an incredible wife/friend, Dorothy, and three absolutely outstanding daughters, Ruth, Joy, and Lindsay.

Truth is, giving thanks isn't very difficult when you enjoy your life's work as much as I do. Being pastor of the The First Presbyterian Church of the Catfish Capital of the World is a great honor, a challenge at times, but always a blessing for which I give thanks to Almighty God.

Every time I have the privilege of waking up to a new day here in the heart of the Mississippi Delta, I give thanks. Each time I can witness the beauty of this land and its people which God has blessed beyond measure, I give thanks. Whenever I go out in the evening on the banks of the Yazoo River and see the heavens which declare the glory of God and the skies which proclaim the work of His hands, I give thanks.

Between Thanksgiving seasons, I cannot count the number of times that people tell me how much such thoughts as these mean to them. Maybe it's a laugh we need. It might even be a shared experience which I happen to touch on.

Whatever I have communicated that has touched some of you, be assured that you and your kind comments mean a great deal to me. When I think of all the remarks and the good-natured ribbing, I give thanks.

I truly hope that being thankful and giving thanks this Thanksgiving will not be a long shot for you, but...

Whatever you do, don't be afraid to go with the long shots. Live life to its fullest every moment and be ready!

"Do not withhold good from those to whom it is due, when it is in the power of your hand to do so." (Proverbs 3:27)

IT DOES A BODY GOOD

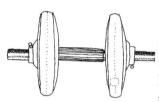 No doubt, some will think that I speak with tongue in cheek, maybe even with forked tongue, but I firmly believe that hunting season each November does a whole lot of good. It's good for the health and productivity of our great nation. If some astute economist would do a study of the matter, I'm convinced that the study would uncover some startling facts.

As a somewhat superficial observer of the economy of the Mississippi Delta, it has been my suspicion that a mild economic recovery occurs about mid-November each year. Just check with the local sporting goods outlets. Go by and ask the good folks at the grocery stores if business doesn't suddenly "boom" at this time of year.

"Thank you," to those who love the outdoors, the thrill of a deer hunt, the comradery of camp life, and who tend to spend quite a bit on their passion during this time of year. Local communities, the state, and the federal government all enjoy tax revenues generated by hunters—a little matter that's overlooked in the hallowed halls of Congress these days as our elected officials daily damn the National Rifle Association and all us blood-thirsty buffoons of the woods and haunts of nature. They want our money, but they want to outlaw our weapons and our ammunition. Well people, you can't have both!

Oops! I forgot myself for a minute there in the heat of the thought of all the calls for gun control, gun bans, and 1000% increase in the tax on ammunition. Everyone already knows how nuts those folks get when they get inside the Washington, D.C. beltway, often defined as six square miles surrounded by reality.

Back to the good that hunting season does for the country. Not only does it create an economic boon, but it also contributes to marital bliss and religious awakening. Now, I know that some

175

of you are thinking, "He really has lost his mind this time!"

Granted, there are some thoughtless slobs who completely ignore the love of their lives during hunting season. And yes, there are many otherwise fine churchmen who absent themselves consistently from church during deer season, but give me a minute to explain my madness.

In the first place, I know for a fact that, as deer season approaches each fall, many a good husband focuses his full attention on those "honey do's" that he has neglected for nearly a year. Leaky faucets get washers. Burned out lightbulbs finally get replaced. House trim that just needed some Clorox to get rid of the mildew about five years ago, now gets a new coat of paint. Leaves get raked. Houses get winterized. Antifreeze is checked. Tires are rotated. Ladies, see what I'm saying? And to top it all off, that tight-wad suddenly hands you the checkbook and says, "Shop 'til you drop while I'm at camp this week." Now can you argue with my conclusion about the good that deer season does for marriage?

Even if you agree with me on marriage, I bet you're thinking, "Yea, but demonstrating how deer season helps bring about revival in the church is going to be a real long shot." (I just love it when a chapter finally gets you readers to thinking like that!)

Whether this holds true in other denominations or not, I really can't say, but it certainly does in the Presbyterian Church. Everyone knows that Presbyterians are widely known for their great doctrine of procrastination. The cornerstone of the doctrinal beliefs of the Presbyterian Church, procrastination, however, gives way to preparation when deer season comes.

Church secretaries have even noticed the revival and transformation as deer season approaches. Suddenly, sermons are completed weeks in advance. Cards and letters are composed and reports completed much earlier than the usual "eleventh hour." From the dust of inactivity rises a whirlwind of ministerial duties. In the twinkling of an eye, many a pastor and many a church member come flying out of their ruts (no doubt as a result of the shortening days and the amount of sunlight which now strikes the retina, which biologists say brings on the rut in deer).

With "honey do's" done and paperwork all wrapped up, it's off to camp for another round of man's favorite past time, telling stories of bygone days, of the big one that got away, and the hunters who have given us so much joy but now gone away.

Though you may not understand why we love it so, I hope that some of you ladies out there will nevertheless get the good out of deer season. Even benefitting from deer season may be a long shot for you, but...

Whatever you do, don't be afraid to go with the long shots. Live life to its fullest every moment and be ready!

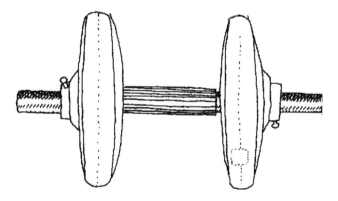

Out of the dead of winter

"Truly God is good to Israel, to such as are pure in heart. But as for me, my feet had almost stumbled; my steps had nearly slipped. For I was envious of the boastful, when I saw the prosperity of the wicked. For there are no pangs in their death, but their strength is firm. They are not in trouble as other men, nor are they plagued like other men." (Psalms 73:1-5)

CONTRASTS

Contrasts, according to the dictionary are differences in color, tone, or emotion which are demonstrated by comparison. Let me illustrate.

Several years ago, the 39-year-old pastor of The First Presbyterian Church of nearby Yazoo City and his young son were killed in an automobile accident. It was New Year's Eve, and the family was returning from a visit with family.

When I received the news by cellular phone at Greasy Bayou, my favorite hunting spot on earth, I was stunned and shocked. Very early the next morning, I sat in the quiet, damp January woods thinking — about the contrast between life and death.

I sat there alive, but part of me had died with my seminary classmate and his young child. Thinking and praying for his family, all I could think about was how senseless their sudden death appeared to be. The contrasts that came to mind as I sat there among the moss-laden oak and cypress trees were staggering.

The forest was quiet, but my heart and mind were in a screaming, swirling turmoil. It was quite a contrast. One minute my eyes and heart would moisten like the mist rising off the adjacent bayou. The next minute, my mind would be charging like a raging bull at the unknown person who caused the wreck.

It was quite a contrast. The forest, on the one hand, proclaimed the sovereign control of a loving God. He obviously cares for the birds of the air and the spike buck that I let walk right past me without raising the rifle.

On the other hand, the picture of my friend and fellow pastor covered by a sheet in a wrecked car stirred my soul. Again, I fought with the same questions we all fight with at such a time.

179

"Why Mike? Why his young son? It's too soon, isn't it God? Surely you weren't through with him, were you?"

It was quite a contrast; the forest so full of life, Mike gone. High above, mallards were calling to their cousins in the slough. Two gobblers strolled by, nibbling acorns. Three squirrels played chase in a nearby tree. An owl hooted his last question of the morning before taking a nap.

But I sat there — with the contrast between death and life on my mind. Mike Sartelle and his youngest son are dead. Their work on earth for their Lord and mine is done.

By contrast, I'm alive and must rise from the quiet of the forest and return to the whirling realities of life. It was quite a contrast.

Contrasts — bring life into focus. While death invades our small worlds all too often, life goes on. And so must we.

Life may be full of confusing contrasts for you too, and these contrasts may make living in the shadow of death a long shot for you, but...

Whatever you do, don't be afraid to go with the long shots. Live life to its fullest every moment and be ready!

"You are the light of the world. A city set on a hill cannot be hidden. Nor do they light a lamp and put it under a basket, but on a lampstand, and it gives light to all who are in the house. Let your light so shine before men, that they may see your good works and glorify your Father in heaven." (Matthew 5:14-16)

THE LIGHT

Like so many other blessings we enjoy in this life, light is something we rarely stop to think about. We aren't grateful for light until something happens and we're suddenly left in the dark.

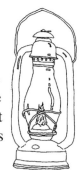

As a child, my mother taught me a funny little story to help me overcome my fear of the dark. She would ask, "Where was Moses when the lights went out? I would answer, "Standing in the corner with his shirttail out."

The humorous mental picture of Moses, the great leader of Israel, standing in a dark corner with his shirttail hanging out helped me to laugh at the dark. Truth is, though, I still don't care too much for the dark.

Like I was saying, we don't appreciate many of the blessings God gives us until something happens and we don't have them anymore. The Lord gave me a good lesson in being thankful for light one very dark November night.

Whenever I can, I like to combine work with pleasure, so during hunting season, I often schedule a hunt around business meetings or hospital visits.

One November morning, I left town with all my hunting gear packed in the front seat of my Toyota truck. After making a couple of hospital visits in Jackson, I planned on driving over to Vicksburg, then north on Highway 61 to Greasy Bayou Hunting Camp, the most beautiful and relaxing place on earth for me.

It was late in the afternoon when I finished visiting with those who were ailing, so I knew nightfall would catch me somewhere on the road.

Over the past year or so, I'd been having some trouble with the headlights on the truck. Sometimes, for no apparent reason, the lights would begin to flicker and then go out completely. At one point, I had to park the truck for several months while I sought help in diagnosing and curing the problem.

The wiring was checked, checked, and rechecked. I felt like I was playing chess or something. No use. We never found a short or anything. Then one day, they began to work again. Miracles do happen, you know.

After months and months of working faithfully, the lights flickered ever so lightly, as I started out of the hospital parking garage. It was such a brief quiver I thought maybe I had imagined it.

A few blocks down the street, they flickered again. I had a knot in my stomach that any Boy Scout would have been proud of. The thought of the lights going out on the way didn't do much for my digestion. This wouldn't have bothered me so much, except for the fact that I hadn't eaten all day.

With my stomach churning like an old ringer washer, and the lights flickering and fluttering like an agitated humming bird, I drove on. By the time I reached the Yazoo River bridge on Highway 61, just ten miles from my destination, darkness had descended totally and completely. Just as the tires clunked on the edge of the bridge, the lights went out.

No, they didn't flicker. They went OUT! "Oh, Lord," I cried, "Where did you say Moses was?"

On a cloudy, moonless night, the darkness is thicker than molasses on a winter day. It's thicker than taffy. If I'd had a knife, it sure wouldn't have cut it.

A half mile beyond the bridge, I found the first place to pull off the highway (which spot I found by the lights of an on-coming car).

The light went on in my brain. "Just get your spotlight out and use it to drive by." What a genius, don't you agree?

There's one problem when great ideas quickly pop up. Sometimes they don't work, which was the case I found with my spotlight—it didn't work. All I had left was a five-cell Brinkman flashlight. You haven't lived until you've driven ten miles on a two-lane highway with a five-cell flashlight. It's like trying to find your way in a coal mine with a single match.

When I turned into the shop at Valley Park, I gave lots of thanks to the good Lord. I got out, phoned home, then got back in the truck to drive on over to camp, which was still two miles down a narrow semi-gravel road. I dreaded those remaining two miles more than you can imagine.

Jumping back in the truck, I turned on the headlights, which hadn't worked in ten miles. They worked! Perfectly! I almost undid my Sunday school lesson, but the thought of God's good keeping on the highway kept me in check.

A few minutes with my favorite electrician, Mr. Ed, the next week, and the problem has been fixed ever since. Would you believe a loose wire?

Driving safely in the dark with no headlights is definitely a long shot I hope never to repeat, but...

Whatever you do, don't be afraid to go with the long shots. Live life to its fullest every moment and be ready!

"But a mist went up from the earth and watered the whole face of the ground." (Genesis 2:6)

BLACK POWDER PERFORMER

A muzzleloader rifle or shotgun is the weapon of choice for many Mississippi hunters about halfway through the annual deer season. At least, muzzleloaders are the weapons the law says must be used for ten days or so in early December.

To tell you the truth, after hunting with the things for about fifteen years now, I'm amazed that the European settlers survived all those encounters with hostile Indians, charging bears, and stalking mountain lions. Though I'm not too good a shot with a modern centerfire rifle, I'm worse with a smokepole. When I shoot these primitive weapons, I give new meaning to the old expression, "hit or miss."

For those who've never had the privilege of hunting with one, shooting one, or even seeing one, let me share a few details about the way they work.

To load a muzzleloader rifle, one must first fire off a few caps in order to be sure the barrel has no moisture in it. Black powder and water are a bad mix. If powder gets the least bit damp, it won't ignite.

After the barrel is dried, the powder is measured out and poured down it. Then a greased rifle bullet or patched roundball (your choice) is placed in the end of the barrel and pushed down on top of the powder charge by means of a long stick called a ramrod.

Once powder and bullet are situated (seated in the breech end of the barrel), the nipple is capped with a small primer. When the hunter lets the hammer down by pulling the trigger, the cap fires. This ignites the charge of powder in the pan which, in turn, sends a spark into the breech of the rifle, setting off the main powder charge. The resulting tumultuous explosion sends the bullet flying on its merry way, which in my case, is known only to the good Lord.

The explosion from firing a black powder rifle is awesome. It's a tremendous, deafening roar followed by a cascade of smoke. Burning black powder tastes and smells a lot like rotten eggs. For a few seconds, it's gross! As you can imagine, Dorothy really loves it when I clean my rifles in her kitchen sink!

Now that you understand the details of loading and firing one of these "primitive weapons," let me take you on a hunt. Here's the fun part.

With rifles loaded (yes, I take two), I ease into my tree stand before daylight. Quietly, I wait for the dawning of a new day. The ground is frozen. The frost has everything looking like my children got loose with a few thousand cans of artificial snow. The temperature is below freezing, and thankfully, the wind is calm.

Birds start to flit about here and there. A couple of squirrels jump from tree to tree; a chipmunk steals a few acorns which a helpful squirrel hid the day before.

Suddenly, I hear a limb breaking. The steps are methodical, too methodical. Somebody's walking in on me. I can't believe it. Nobody else is supposed to be here!"

I'm just about ready to preach my Sunday sermon in reverse when I spot the source of the steps. It isn't a man at all. It's a very nice 8-point buck! He's nearly a hundred yards away, coming in my direction.

As he draws closer and closer, the muzzleloader is still resting on my lap, half-cocked (that's the safety position). He's within thirty yards and stops to tear the top out of a honeysuckle vine, oblivious to the danger as he chomps on his snack.

I see some scars on his neck. He's been fighting with other bucks for the attention of the ladies. His horns have bark stuck in them near the base of his brow tines. He's been rubbing trees all around his home territory as part of the mating and fighting ritual of the rut.

His tail twitches slightly like a leaf being tossed by a gentle breeze. He reaches back to nibble at something itching his hind

185

quarter. While his head is turned away from me, I ease the rifle to my shoulder.

With the hammer now at full cock, I place the bead of the front sight directly behind his shoulder. He straightens up just as I squeeze the trigger.

"Kabloooooom!" Smoke and rotten egg smells fill the air. I listen for some kind of commotion. There's nothing but silence.

As the smoke drifts away, I look and behold — the deer is still standing, looking heavenward. He may be praying or maybe "just thinking" that it either thundered or the stinkingest fog in history has settled in his part of the woods. Then, the deer looks up directly into my eyes and shakes his head up and down a couple of times. I believe I can read his mind. He's saying, "Thank you, Lord. The preacher is hunting with his muzzleloader again!"

Hitting the mark with a muzzleloading rifle is honestly a long shot for me. Maybe it is for you, too, but...

Whatever you do, don't be afraid to go with the long shots. Live life to its fullest every moment and be ready!

"Where there is no counsel, the people fall; But in the multitude of counselors there is safety." (Proverbs 11:14)

INPUT

Just as "inland" means "in land from the sea or the Mexican border," so "input," the dictionary says, means "to put in." Makes sense, doesn't it?

Several times during February each year, the Mississippi Department of Wildlife, Fisherie and Parks holds open meetings across the state to receive "input" from Mississippi's hunters and fishermen. "A mighty nice idea," I thought to myself.

Having seen an announcement in the local paper as per the time and place of said "input" meeting, I grabbed my AVR (Automatic Voice-activated Recorder) and set off for the meeting place at the appointed hour.

Though I'm sure that other meetings across the state were well-attended (at least that's what the men in the green uniforms said), the one I attended wasn't.

We waited until several millennium past the witching hour before the meeting started, ostensibly waiting on the late-comers to show. (They never did!)

I looked around the room at those of us present to give our "input." There were some forty officials of the State and eleven of us civilians, one of whom I recognized as a retired federal game warden.

Those who registered at the door were asked their name and address and whether or not we wished to make comments or ask questions. I put down that I didn't wish to say anything, thinking that we would have a good crowd, with lots of people asking lots of questions and offering all kinds of comments — "input," don't you see?

Well, I think three of us finally asked a few questions and made a few comments about such matters as the good job that's been done stocking Delta lakes, the bag limit on deer, the length of seasons on deer, rabbits, etc. The dramatic decline in deer, quail, and rabbit populations in the Delta was also discussed.

After we provided our two cents' worth of "input," we sat back and listened to what the powers that be had to say. We were jokingly told that with so few of us present, the Department could just tell us what it was going to do and be done with it. It was a joke, but there was all too much truth in that comment.

I'm not knocking the Department. They do a fine job with the little resources and support they receive from us outdoorsmen. The sad truth is, because so few of us act like we care (as was evidenced by the small turnout), the Department of Wildlife has no choice but go on their best judgment.

As a sportsman, I think we should all do our part to insure the future of hunting and fishing in our great nation. Few places on earth have the diverse natural beauty and abundance of game that ours does. Folks, if we who love to hunt and fish don't get more involved in the process, we won't have the privilege much longer. Some left-field ecologist will have us all sitting cross-legged, eating beansprouts!

Some of you might think it's a long shot for your opinions to be heard at the public meetings held each year by the state departments of wildlife, but then, how many of us are afraid to go with a long shot now and then?

Whatever you do, don't be afraid to go with the long shots. Live life to its fullest every moment and be ready!

"Yet He had commanded the clouds above, and opened the doors of heaven, had rained down manna on them to eat, and given them of the bread of heaven. Men ate angels' food; He sent them food to the full." (Psalms 78:23-25)

NOW WE'RE COOKING!

The invasion of successive cold fronts brought our beautiful Indian Summer to an abrupt end. All those warm, sometimes hot, sunny days were mighty nice, but not characteristic of November and the opening of gun season for deer.

In a few short weeks, trucks laden with people, packages, and paraphernalia would be all over the highway. The hum of mud grip tires on four wheel drive vehicles would soon drown out the occasional passage of flocks of geese floating along overhead in the darkness of the night sky.

Every imaginable size, shape, and color of camper trailers and four-wheelers dot the roadways of the Magnolia State at this time of year. It's always amazing to me to look at truck tags and see where folks are from.

People from the Delta flatlands are always headed to the hills, and people from the hills are headed to the Delta. I often wonder why they don't get together and swap hunting lands so they can hunt closer to home. But then I guess an important part of going to deer camp is getting away from home and the telephone. What do you think?

One of the great things about the first deer season with guns and dogs is camp life. Most hunting camps don't really get cranked up until the weekend before Thanksgiving. For the next week to ten days, life in camp is one tale and meal after another. People who don't crack a smile from January to the middle of November split their sides laughing at the same stories they've heard for decades. Deer camp is just plain good for folks' attitudes.

If deer camp is good for people's emotional well-being, it's kind of rough on their physical conditioning. All the time spent sitting in deer stands, relaxing around the camp telling stories, and sitting at the table takes its toll on the girth. Most of us over forty start to dwindle away to enormity during the Thanksgiving and

Christmas hunts.

For years I've tried to figure out what makes food taste so good at camp. Even the simplest meal has an enhanced flavor when it's consumed among hunting buddies at camp.

Perhaps some of you wives have been frustrated by all the tales about how good camp food is. Probably got your feelings hurt a time or too as well. Let me see if I can help.

Now mind you, men, my help may backfire on some of you who are beyond help anyway. When it comes to an angry wife, one who has really jumped hot at you, "Only you can prevent forest fires!" Well, here goes my attempt to smooth things over at your house.

Ladies — doesn't food cooked by someone else always seem to taste better? When someone else has to wash all those filthy pots, pans, and dishes, and clean off the table, doesn't the food just taste better? I would ask you if food cooked in a restaurant doesn't taste better, but I'm afraid your hunter/husband hasn't taken you out lately! (Remember, I'm just trying to help, guys.) But you get my drift, don't you?

It's the same with camp food. It isn't that the cooks are better at camp. Just as you have experienced yourself, food cooked somewhere else by someone else and shared with people you genuinely like always tastes better.

Given the fact that venison cooked at camp mysteriously tastes better than when cooked at home, let me suggest a truly tasty recipe for venison roast from an unusual cookbook by the title, Outdoor Table and Tales, by the Southeastern Outdoor Press Association. Hope you like it!

Venison Roast

The following recipe represents 10-12 servings. The ingredients are:

1 3-5 lb. venison roast
1/4 cup all purpose flour
1/4 cup firmly packed brown sugar
1 tsp paprika
1/2 tsp black pepper
6 TBSP butter

1/2 cup venison or beef broth

2 stalks celery, chopped

1 onion, chopped

10 onions, quartered (optional)

10 potatoes, quartered (optional)

Blend flour, brown sugar, and seasonings and sprinkle over meat. Saute' meat in butter using a dutch oven, turning to brown all sides. Add broth, celery, and chopped onion. Bake, covered at 375 degrees for 3 1/2 to 4 hours, adding potatoes and onions to bake during the final thirty minutes. (Recipe comes from Uncle Russ Chittenden of Padukah, Kentucky.)

Outdoor Tables and Tales is more than your run-of-the-mill cookbook. It is, as its title suggests, filled with great stories, lots of humor, and some great reminders of special days spent hunting and fishing. Check with your local bookstore for what could very well save your marriage or be a great Christmas gift for the love of your life.

Cooking venison or any of the other delicious recipes from Outdoor Tables and Tales so that it tastes just like it would at deer or duck camp may be a long shot for you, but...

Whatever you do, don't be afraid to go with the long shots. Live life to its fullest every moment and be ready!

"Now the King of Syria had commanded the thirty-two captains of his chariots, saying, 'Fight with no one small or great, but only with the King of Israel.' So it was, when the captains of the chariots saw Jehoshaphat, that they said, 'Surely it is the king of Israel!' Therefore they turned aside to fight against him, and Jehoshaphat cried out. And it happened, when the captains of the chariots saw that it was not the king of Israel, that they turned back from pursuing him." (I Kings 22:31-33)

A CASE OF MISTAKEN IDENTITY

No doubt, you've heard of mistaken identities. You know, people being mistaken for someone else. Mamma always said, "Son, they say that somewhere in this ole world there's somebody who's just like somebody else. Oh, Lord! Tell me it ain't so in YOUR case!"

As a result, as you can well imagine, I've been marked for life. Why, I'm so shy and reserved I get upset when I meet myself in the mirror! Now, there you go reading things into this article again. I know what you're thinking.

"If I had to look at that face in the mirror, I'd get real quiet too!"

Enough of that. Let me do the writing. You just stick to reading.

Well, getting back to mistaken identities and all that. One fall, at our deer camp in Holmes County, we enjoyed one of our best deer/member ratios ever. Several of us took two or more nice ones.

A couple of our members weren't in on much of this success though. (I'll not mention their names to protect the unfortunate and their often neglected families.) These two fellows had hunted hard, though unsuccessfully.

Finally, during muzzleloader season, one of our other members killed a small deer. Ernest and Leon Cobb watched as he cleaned the deer, left it hanging on the rack, and went into town. After the successful hunter left, so did Ernest and Leon. This is where the plot thickens. The first hunter returned, loaded his deer into his truck and went on back home.

The deerless member who teaches science at Mississippi

192

Delta Community College and lives in Indianola with his wife, college-age son, and young daughter (I said I wouldn't mention their names, remember?) killed a small buck. Having cleaned his kill, he left it hanging on the skinning rack and went back to the woods.

In the mean time, Ernest and Leon came in to rest for a while. Hunting is hard work, don't you see?

About that same time, the other unsuccessful hunter, the one who works for the Mississippi Highway Department and lives next door to Calvary Baptist Church just outside Belzoni, came in. Not having killed a deer, he was really hungry for some meat. I personally think that his wife was questioning his whereabouts all those weekends, because he never took any deer meat home.

Not being privy to the information that two very similar deer had been killed, Ernest and Leon told the forlorn hunter, "Bubba must've left his deer because he didn't want it. Why don't you just take it home with you?"

Delighted by everyone's generosity, he loaded up the deer and left immediately. That deer was like the key to the front door. His wife had threatened to change the locks if he didn't bring home some meat!

When the professor came in, his deer was gone. "Okay guys, what did ya'll do with my deer?"

"Your deer?" the two surprised Cobb's responded. "What do you mean, YOUR DEER?"

The look on the doctor's face said it all. It was a case of mistaken identity, pure and simple.

When the highway robber learned that his game was up, he was horrified. "I woulda never took it if I'd just known."

"Yeah, sure." Wishing to keep a good joke going, I suggested he send a thank-you note to the professor.

"That ain't funny."

"Okay then, I'll send him one for you and put your return address on it. I'll even send him a couple of extra bullets and tell him, `Get me another one!' I think I'll even suggest he send you the key to his trailer. You might as well sleep in his bed and eat his food if you're gonna swipe his meat."

193

The weeping and wailing and gnashing of teeth could be heard all over that hillside. Mistaken identities can be terrible.

I hope that an unfortunate case of mistaken identity will be a long shot for you, but...

Whatever you do, don't be afraid to go with the long shots. Live life to its fullest every moment and be ready!

"How the mighty have fallen in the midst of battle!"

(II Samuel 1:25a)

THE BLUFF

One of my favorite movies in recent years is "The Gambler" with Kenny Rogers as the main character. As the song goes, "You got to know when to hold 'em, know when to fold 'em, know when to walk away, and know when to  run . . ." The point of all this movie nostalgia is that the gambler knew how to run a bluff.

Since I could never stand the thought of losing money at cards, I was never involved in a poker game (not even penny poker!), but I've watched a game or two. One thing's for sure, if you're going to play poker, you better know how to bluff.

Sometime back, several of my hunting buddies out in the hills gave Joe Lloyd a lesson in running a bluff. The story began long before daylight one morning as Ed Cobb, Hoggie Hargraves, and Joe Lloyd were riding to their deer stands in Ed's truck.

The headlights of the Ford pickup were dancing around like fireflies as they bounced down the rutted logging road to the backside of nowhere. As the truck rolled to a stop, the beam from the truck lights illuminated a kudzu patch and one very prominent large water oak tree.

From inside the cab of the truck, the kudzu looked like green carpet that kept on going a good ways past the tree. Though two of the pickup occupants knew otherwise, they inadvertently failed to fill the third mate in on one minor detail.

"What was that?" you ask.

The kudzu patch and the lone oak were on the edge of a deep bluff. Even though some of the leafy vine ran out past the tree, the ground didn't!

Joe got out and reached for the 12-foot ladder stand in the back of the pickup. Walking to the back of the truck, he now

195

recalls, he wondered why Ed and Hoggie were both laughing so hard that the truck was vibrating. Knowing them, he figured one of them had said or done something that tickled the other one. On he went, not realizing that he was about to run a bluff far beyond The Gambler's abilities.

According to testimony from the two truck tricksters, the moment Joe walked around the backside of the tree to raise the tree stand, he simply disappeared. WHUUUMPH! There he went. Gone from sight.

"Where'd he go?" Hog asked as if he didn't know.

"Beats me, but we better go check on him."

Rushing up to the edge of the 40-foot bluff, Ed and Hog shined their flashlights into the deep darkness. There was Joe, clinging to a kudzu vine, wearing that deer stand like a conduit necklace.

"Joe, are you all right?"

Never mind the response they got to that question. I'm glad to report that he was shaken but not hurt. Now you might imagine that at this point, Joe's "friends" would have helped him out of his predicament, but NOOOO...

While Joe clung precariously to the creeping hillside curse, Ed and Hog were on their knees — laughing — choking — gasping for air. Finally, when they could gain their feet again, they pulled Joe to safety and swore they didn't know the bluff was there.

After years of sticking to their story, Hoggie finally let it slip the other night that Ed was the mastermind behind the whole plot. He was only along for the ride that morning. Now who's trying to run a bluff?

Running a bluff in a poker game or running off a bluff in a kudzu patch might be a long shot for you (I sure hope both are), but...

Whatever you do, don't be afraid to go with the long shots. Live life to its fullest every moment and be ready!

"Then I will shoot three arrows to the side of it, as though I shot at a target." (I Samuel 20:20)

KNIGHTS, BUT NOT IN SHINING ARMOR

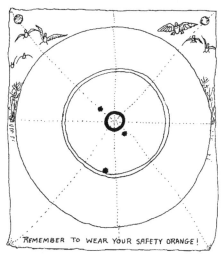

REMEMBER TO WEAR YOUR SAFETY ORANGE!

Out at the target range the other day, the muzzleloader rifle I was firing wasn't consistent at all. The first round struck the target six inches low and three inches to the left. After adjusting the sight and reloading, I fired off another booming round. This time the bullet hit two inches high and two inches left. Another cycle of realigning the sight and gearing up for another shot followed, with the frustrating result of two inches low and an inch right!

Being prepared is something we try to instill in our Boy Scouts, and I take it to heart myself when it comes to hunting with what is described as a "modern muzzleloader." So, without becoming too frustrated, I whipped out my back-up rifle, loaded her up and fired off a charge of blackpowder and buffalo bullet. Though I had some three feet of target to shoot at, the sight was so off on the second rifle, the round hit the ground. So did the rifle!

Domestically at home trimming the Christmas tree that evening, I casually mentioned to Dorothy that a new muzzleloader was all I wanted for Christmas this year. After an appropriate amount of time to allow the wish to be processed in her non-hunting memory banks, I offered to save her the trouble of shopping for one. "Since the season is open now, why don't I just go ahead and get my present? I can wrap up the box and put it under the tree."

Like a professional politician, there was no response from said spouse. Naturally, from my teenage experiences when I quietly asked for permission to go somewhere I shouldn't be going (yes, I can still remember that far back!), I concluded that no comment was an affirmative.

Later that evening, after running the clock at the basketball game, Ernest Cobb and I made a little excursion to one of our local gun shops. Having been in this establishment on several other occasions to browse, I knew the proprietor kept a good stock of all types of firearms. In a matter of seconds, my desired weapon was in sight, which after the experience trying to sight in the other rifles on the range, made the sale imminent.

Without even asking what the price was, I said, "I want that Knight Legend rifle, the one with the camo stock and I want one of those laser dot sights on it." When he handed me the rigged up rifle, I was amazed at the price, much less than I had expected. Relieved that it wouldn't take a diamond ring or a full-length fur to match the purchase, Ernest and I headed to deer camp.

Like a kid waiting for Santa on Christmas Eve, I could hardly wait to see and try out my new toy. With the most accurate rifle and best sighting system in hand, I was assured of catching up with Ruth, who happened to be the only member of the Wiman family to have gotten a deer that season.

We slept late the next morning because a deluge that came during the night was still falling at daylight. By noon, the weather had broken, but a stiff northwest wind had sprung up. The wind came in waves like the rolling tide, blowing so hard the ground seemed to shake. Regal oaks bent nearly to the breaking point, and young pines reached down brushing the ground like an umpire waving the safe sign.

"There's no way I'm gonna see a deer under these conditions," I mused. Unseen, out in the forest, came the sound of a deer walking. Closer and closer it came, appearing like an apparition from the wooded hollow in front of me. Turning broadsided to me at 20 yards, I aimed the red dot at the deer's shoulder and fired away.

When the smoke cleared, one amused deer trotted off laughing, obviously having read *Tired Tubes and Ten-Speed Turkeys* and the chapter about how I ALWAYS miss the first shot with a muzzleloader!

No matter how "high tech" we hunters become, the poor, innocent deer still have a better chance of getting run over by some liberal, bleeding-heart, anti-hunter behind the wheel of a speeding car than getting killed by those of us who hunt with muzzleloader rifles.

Receiving a Christmas gift that won't miss the mark might be a long shot for you, and though it is...

Whatever you do, don't be afraid to go with the long shots. Live life to its fullest every moment and be ready!

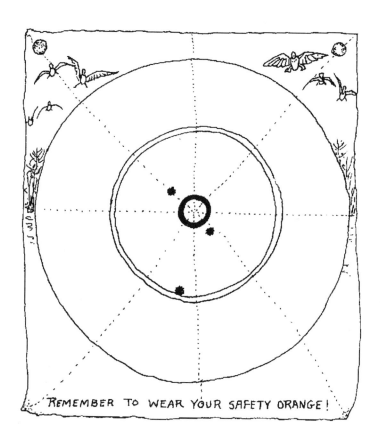

REMEMBER TO WEAR YOUR SAFETY ORANGE!

"A false witness will not go unpunished, and he who speaks lies will not escape."(Proverbs 19:5)

THE BIG ONE GOT AWAY ... AGAIN

Do you ever wonder why the big one always seems to get away? It doesn't matter whether it's a bass, a deer, or a business deal, the big one always turns out to be as elusive as snow in Jamaica.

Don't think that I'm being skeptical or anything about the big one getting away. The Lord knows that I've had my share of almosts.

There was the time I was fishing in a farm pond with some of my college buddies. The fellow on either side of me landed a couple of really nice fish, five to six pounders.

By the end of the day, I had tried the exact same lures and cast in the same type spots, but to no avail. The picture of the stringer full of huge bass I helped hold up (but not catch) was ample evidence that, once again, the big one had gotten away. So much for the big one!

Of course, there was the time I was deer hunting down at Reed Deer Camp, on the banks of the Mississippi River. It was the last day of the season and COLD! The horse riders announced their plan of attack, so I took off to put my stand up in a likely spot.

No sooner had I settled down on my ten-foot ladder stand than a beautiful ten-point buck stepped out of the thick woods into a wide open turnrow. What an awesome deer! Gawking through the scope at the wall hanger standing less than 100 yards away, I caught myself admiring the size of the horns and the spread instead of taking a shot.

The .270 roared as it had on several previous occasions that season, but with far different results than I had expected. Instead of dropping in his tracks, the monster buck bounded off into the cottonwoods and left me with nothing but a gaping mouth, an incredulous look, and another chapter for this book.

After a few moments, I realized I had never sighted in on the deer. I was still aiming the rifle somewhere amongst the antlers when I pulled the trigger. So much for the big one! I don't know why it is, but the big ones always seem to get away from me.

To tell you the truth, I thought I had used and/or heard about every excuse in the book for the big one getting away, until a certain person with PCA Credit here in Belzoni stopped by the church one morning to tell me his version/excuse/baloney, whatever you want to call it.

I can honestly say that I've never heard a more colorful explanation of how the big one got away. This great hunter supposedly killed his second spike buck of the archery season. After lifting the deer onto the rack of his three-wheeler, he drove through the woods to his pickup. The three-wheeler, deer and all, was then loaded onto the tricycle trailer for the short drive to his house. He says he wanted to show his young son the deer.

Somewhere along the highway, however, is where the story gets a bit murky. It seems that the three-wheeler, deer and all, mysteriously unloaded itself while our happy hunter was driving down the four-lane, well-travelled road.

After being stopped by a following motorist and told of the awful occurrence, he returned to find his three-wheeler on the side of the road — unscathed — but deerless!

"Somebody stole my deer!" he bemoaned while shuffling his feet, eyes downcast.

"It's no wonder somebody stole it," I interjected unsympathetically into his melancholy mood. "But what I don't understand is why they took the deer. They should have stolen the three-wheeler. It had a better rack than the scrawny ole deer!"

If any of you have a story about the one that got away that can beat the self-unloading, deer-losing three-wheeler, please let me know. I don't promise I'll believe you, but I might just write about you anyway, huh, Clark?

Because of our scripture text for this chapter, we all ought to think twice about trying to top Clark Patterson's story. But even if resisting the temptation to tell a tale about the big one that got away again is a long shot for you...

Whatever you do, don't be afraid to go with the long shots. Live life to its fullest every moment and be ready!

"And their father Israel said to them, `If it must be so, then do this: take some of the best fruits of the land in your vessels and carry down a present for the man—a little balm and a little honey, spices and myrrh, pistachio nuts and almonds."(Genesis 43:11)

NUTS

One of my favorite commercial tunes through the years has been the Almond Joy candy lyric. "Sometimes you feel like a nut; sometimes you don't. Almond Joy has nuts.  Mounds don't, cause - sometimes you feel like a nut — sometimes you don't!"

I think the reason I've always liked that tune so much is because it really describes me. Sometimes I feel like a nut; sometimes I don't. One of the joys of being an outdoors person is that sometimes when I feel like it, I can be a nut when no one else is around. Before you take off on the thought that just ran through your mind, I will freely admit that the nuttier side has sometimes slipped out with other humans around.

In case you haven't noticed lately, nuts are everywhere. Now, now, I'm not talking about those people whose elevator doesn't go all the way to the top floor or those folks who aren't playing with a full deck, nor those who are a few bricks short of a full load. No, I'm talking about the acorns that are so popular with local wildlife.

When most city slickers think of acorns, only the bushytailed high-rise rodent known as the squirrel comes to mind. Truth is, not only do squirrels love acorns, but so do just about every other species of bird and mammal in the area. Chipmunks love acorns, but prefer to steal them from the squirrels! Deer love acorns, especially white oaks. Turkeys love acorns, likewise ducks.

One of the joys of being a hunter and outdoorsman is sitting in the woods during the fall watching all the critters and their love affair with acorns. Such activity and cooperation between different animals and birds is plumb enjoyable.

Squirrels jump from limb to limb, shaking the trees like a

high wind. The little jokers hang by what looks like a mere thread of a limb some forty feet above the forest floor, pull an acorn from its cup, run back to a more secure perch, then sit on their back legs, remove the shell and devour the delicious, sweet meat of the acorn. In a matter of moments, the squirrel races to yet another precarious part of the tree and claims another prize.

Birds often float into the same tree with the squirrels and begin to peck away at an acorn or two. Most of the acorns the birds manage to dislodge fall to the ground, which is mighty kind of them. Deer and turkeys sure appreciate the help. Without the help of birds, high winds and heavy frosts, the deer and turkeys would be like the women on the way to Jesus' tomb on resurrection morning, wondering, "Who will roll away the stone for us?" As the angel rolled away the stone on Easter Sunday morning, so God has provided a way for the deer and turkeys to enjoy the fruit of His great trees — the white, red, and water oaks.

Besides the acorns, squirrels also enjoy hickory nuts. These half-dollar sized nuts are one of the prime food sources for squirrels. A hickory nut chewing fox squirrel can be heard cutting hickory nuts for a hundred yards or more.

I have to confess that I, too, love nuts. My favorites are Dorothy (no, no, just kidding) — cashews and pistachios, though peanuts are more in line with my budget. Quite often, a pocket-full of pistachios helps pass the time as I sit and enjoy the wonderful and nutty outdoors.

Enjoying a nut out in the woods may be a long shot for you, but...

Whatever you do, don't be afraid to go with the long shots. Live life to its fullest every moment and be ready!

"Do not let your left hand know what your right hand is doing."
(Matthew 6:3b)

ONE-HAND WONDERS

"Look, Mom, no hands!" I remember calling out as I flew past our house in Brandon on my new bike. Our driveway was gravel, the hill steep, the red bike all shiny and new, and the pilot of the streaking cycle confident, boastful, a touch arrogant, and definitely cocky.

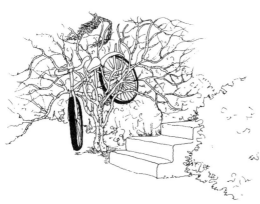

Just as I was proclaiming my prowess and demonstrating my disgusting pride, the whole world turned upside down. I don't know to this day what happened, but all at once the bicycle was riding me. Its guidance system wasn't nearly as reliable as mine. We crashed through the neighbor's hedge, rose bushes, and concrete steps in the flash of an eye.

Mother stood there, mouth agape, apron drawn up about her face, flashing eyes (that's where the flash of an eye came from). Horrified! Terrified! Well, actually, she was wiping tears from her face. She finally admitted years later that she had never laughed so hard in all her life. She had been thinking, "He's gonna get his cocky little keester torn up one of these days," when bike and I exchanged positions.

Though I didn't quit riding with no hands, I did quit calling attention to the fact. After that fateful day, I just sat back with arms folded and rode around like Mr. Joe Cool. (Mr. Jack Fool would be more like it.) Oh, how far the mighty do fall. The cock that crows the loudest and longest usually gets it first!

Anyway, getting back to performing feats with no hands or one hand is something I still love to try.

There was the time I was quail hunting with a man from

205

work who lived out east of Jackson, near the little town of Raymond. He supposedly had a fine birddog. Only problem was, when we fired the first shot, the dog ran home!

We were trying to head the dog off, when we jumped a covey of birds. Quick, stop the truck! I bailed out and over the fence in a single bound. With both feet firmly on the other side of the fence, I loaded my shotgun, but time was of the essence. A single bird burst from beneath my feet just as I was loading the shell into the chamber. Since I had a handful of shells in one hand and the shotgun in the other, I tried a one-handed shot. Guess what?

Yep, I killed it. Just like Bubba shot the jukebox, I stopped that quail with one, one-handed shot. I was so proud of myself. I retrieved the bird, turned toward my friend, holding up the gun in one hand and the quail in the other and said, "Not bad, huh?"

I won't repeat what he said about me. Let's just go on to the now famous rabbit hunt. Every time I turned around on that particular hunt, the dogs were running a rabbit by me. I had just killed a rabbit and bent over to pick it up when the dogs jumped another rabbit and ran it by me as well. With deceased rabbit in one hand and shotgun in the other, I turned and rolled the second rabbit with one shot.

I was so proud of myself. I retrieved my other rabbit, turned toward my friends, and holding the gun up in one hand and the two rabbits in the other, said: "Not bad, huh?"

I won't repeat what they said about me either! Let's just go on to the next episode, a duck hunt.

Dick Taylor, his son, Tom, and I were in a small duck boat in a break near Tunica. The mallards were falling in all around, and Dick was trying to maneuver me for a shot.

The duck boat wasn't turning fast enough to allow the gun to come to bear on the two ducks that were approaching. I turned and aimed the 3-inch magnum over and under 12 gauge shotgun with one hand. I even picked out the greenhead instead of the hen! BALOOOM! One mallard for lunch, thank you.

"Wow, Dad, did you see Mr. Richard shoot that duck with one hand?" I won't repeat what Dick said, but it was nice for someone else to do the bragging for once! Thanks, Tom Taylor!

Then on a recent squirrel hunt, it happened again. I was riding a very tall horse, so tall I had to find a stump to mount him in the first place. For this reason, I never got off the horse all afternoon long.

Every time the dogs treed a squirrel, I tried to position the horse so I could shoot if one appeared on my side of the tree. On this one occasion I wasn't able to do so before a squirrel came barrelling around my side of the tree. With one hand, I raised the 20 gauge, aimed, and fired. As the squirrel dropped, I caught the shotgun with my other hand. The recoil had knocked the gun clean out of my right hand and into my left hand!

While I was calling everyone's attention to my amazing feat, a second limb rat emerged and raced up my side of the tree. I fired again with my left hand, but with my right behind the butt plate to prevent a second attempt at escape by the weapon. The result was the same as the first, a falling squirrel.

I was so proud of myself. "Not bad, huh?" At that very moment, a third squirrel came tearing out, and with both hands on the gun, I fired at the easiest shot of the day, and missed completely! How far the proud can fall in just a matter of seconds.

Making one-hand shots may be a long shot for you. Making one hand-shots and remaining humble may be an even longer shot for you, but...

Whatever you do, don't be afraid to go with the long shots. Live life to its fullest every moment and be ready!

"I know how to be abased, and I know how to abound. Everywhere and in all things I have learned both to be full and to be hungry, both to abound and to suffer need. I can do all things through Christ who strengthens me." (Phillippians 4:12-13)

THE DELTA DIFFERENCE

When my family and I moved to the Mississippi Delta at the end of 1981, we wondered what life would be like in another country. You see, we came to the Delta from the hills and hollers of Smith County, located in the southcentral part of the state.

"Life in the flatlands," we were warned, "is vastly different from the life you're used to here in the hills." They were correct, but the truly amazing element of their assessment lies in the fact that at one time or another, we all came from the hills!

Less than 200 years ago, a few scattered Indian tribes were the only human beings who dared face the test of surviving in this humid, mosquito and snake-infested flood plain. If the numerous bears or panthers didn't get them, malaria would. If malaria or some other tropical disease didn't get them, the annual spring floods would. The Indian mounds which are found throughout the Delta are testimony to the Indians' efforts to beat the odds and survive in this region. A quick perusal of the local phone books for familiar Indian names will tell you, though, that something got the Indians after all.

Anyway, when the rest of us started sliding out of the hills and taking up residence in this rich, alluvial delta plain, our way of life took a definite turn from what it had been like in the hills. Our way of life here in the Mississippi Delta is certainly divergent from that of the hillbillies we left behind.

For example, I never met a hill farmer who was going broke in the showroom of the local Lincoln Continental dealership purchasing a new car for his wife. Neither have I ever checked out a dove hunting site in a Lincoln anywhere else but the Delta.

Life is different in the Delta. Hunting camps in the Delta tend to be built differently as well. While some will, no doubt, resemble their hill counterparts, for the most part they're as distinct from one another as daylight from dark.

One of my old-time deer hunting partners related this experience. He was invited to go to a deer camp in the hills for a few days of some of the finest whitetail hunting and comfortable camp life he'd ever seen.

"What do I need to bring? Sheets, blankets, towels, etc.?"

"Just bring an ole blanket. You won't need any of that other stuff."

When they turned off the highway onto the black top, my buddy expected to see a fine camp house, perched on a low hill, a pond perfectly situated between the house and the road, and an incredible view of the trackless expanse of the Delta. On they drove.

When they turned off the black top onto a gravel county road, he expected to see a fairly nice camp house, partially hidden from the road by a thick stand of pine trees and a smattering of oaks and a persimmon or two to draw the deer right into the yard at night. On they drove.

When the gravel road played out, and then the dirt road played out, and the logging trail narrowed, he was prepared for an old rustic shotgun house with no electricity or running water, a privy out back, and enough space between the floor boards to throw a cat.

Instead, he was greeted by a rusty cotton trailer, which had been turned upside down. Several tattered tarpaulins formed the flimsy walls, and a cutting torch had opened a door in one end.

"Ain't it a beaut?"

"It's something else, all right."

Now, that's a hillbilly deer camp for you.

On the other hand, the nice little cabin up at Catfish Point is the Delta Deer Camp personified. Built on a high bluff overlooking the mighty Father of Waters, this million-dollar facility has all the modern conveniences. Everything you ever wanted, whether you needed it or not, has been provided.

Those who enjoy deer season "roughing it" at Catfish Point clearly demonstrate the difference between the hills and the Delta ways of life.

Most of us, both hillbilly ridge-runners and Delta flatlanders, hunt from a camp somewhere in between the two examples mentioned above. Yes, a microwave, TV/VCR, and central heat and air are welcome additions to the hunting camp of today, both in the hills and here in the Delta.

Enjoying the comforts of a fine Delta hunting camp and the other cultural distinctives of our special section might be a long shot for you, but...

Whatever you do, don't be afraid to go with the long shots. Live life to its fullest every moment and be ready!

"And everyone who competes for the prize is temperate in all things. Now they do it to obtain a perishable crown, but we for an imperishable crown." (I Corinthians 9:25)

TROPHIES

Like most folks, we have a few trophies around our house, tokens of outstanding achievements by first one and then another. As I gaze at these mementos made of metal and marble, I'm reminded of the events, the people, and the feelings which these treasures represent.

On the shelf in my study at church is a baseball trophy. Beside it is a picture, a signed baseball, and a plaque with all the players' names. It was the last Dixie Youth baseball team I coached. Those kids went 17-0 that season. The way some professional teams play each year, I believe my young men could have beaten those over-paid crybabies.

When I look at that trophy, though, it's not the victories that come to mind. It's the boys, the hours we spent practicing, the games we came from behind to win. It's the thought that maybe I've played a part in teaching them the value of hard work and the attitude that nobody is a loser who competes and gives his best until the last out has been recorded. Trophies . . .

Then there are the music awards, the medals, certificates, and the John Philip Sousa Award, things from high school. When I look at those recognitions, both Dorothy's and mine, I'm reminded more of the sacrifices that were made for us to achieve those honors rather than the thrill of the honors themselves. Our mothers spent countless hours and lots of hard-earned dollars to see to it that we had the private lessons we needed to become among the best clarinetists and percussionists in the state. All those medals and awards, the college scholarship that the drums landed me to the University of Southern Mississippi, remind us every day that the hours spent practicing were worth it. We've learned the value of hard work and the attitude that nobody is a loser who competes and gives his best until the last note has been played. Trophies . . .

Trophies the girls won as a result of showing sheep in 4-H decorate our den these days. We're all proud of those ribbons and awards. When I look at those honors, it's not that one or the other of the girls finished first in their class that comes to mind. Those trophies remind me of the hard work and sacrifices that parents, children, and our friends, the Wise family, made in order for us to pass along to the next generation the value of hard work and the attitude that nobody is a loser who competes and gives his best until the judge makes his final decision. Trophies . . .

As I look around the room, I see other trophies. There are several whitetail deer, a pair of bobwhite quail, a black mallard, a greenhead and hen mallard, a large fox squirrel, and a beautiful pheasant. Some of these animals are universally acknowledged as trophies. Others are trophies only in my eyes. Each of these reminds me of exciting hunts and special friends. Each critter is also a testimony to the value of hard work and the attitude that nobody is a loser who competes and gives his best till the sun goes down on the last day of the season. Trophies . . .

The idea for this chapter struck me as I was watching the summer Olympics. One of our swimmers met with tragedy at the games. While he was competing in a qualifying heat, his father had a heart attack and died in the stands. Less than a week later, the young man finished sixth in his race. To my absolute disgust, I heard a commentator ask him if he was disappointed in losing.

"Losing!" I cried to myself. That young man didn't lose. He finished sixth in the world, for goodness sake! He was less than a second behind the young man who finished in first place. Just because he didn't go home with a medal, in the mind of that commentator, he was a loser. How sad. I feel sorry for people in our world who think that only those who win a trophy are winners. Trophies . . .

When some folks look at my mounted deer, they don't see

a trophy animal. To them, a deer has to qualify for Boone and Crockett to be considered a trophy. For me, a trophy is anything that reminds me that I competed, worked hard, and persevered to the end. Trophies . . .

Work hard. Be willing to make sacrifices. Compete. Don't quit until the last out has been recorded, the last note played, the last breath drawn. You'll be a winner, no matter what the world says. Trophies . . .

Winning a World Series, capturing first place in a golf tournament, killing a record-book buck, or being acknowledged by your peers as the best at whatever you do may be a long shot for you, but...

Whatever you do, don't be afraid to go with the long shots. Give it your best shot. Live life to its fullest every moment and be ready!

"But Ruth said, `Entreat me not to leave you, or to turn back from following after you; for wherever you go, I will go; and wherever you lodge, I will lodge; your people shall be my people, and your God, my God. Where you die, I will die, and there I will be buried. The Lord do so to me, and more also, if anything but death parts you and me." (Ruth 1:16-17)

RUTH, YES SHE IS!

This past Friday at deer camp, we were treated to the movie "Dennis the Menace". Normally, we don't have access to a VCR, but in this case, one of the guys brought one. The next morning, I noticed another movie waiting to be viewed, and believe it or not Mr. Ripley, it was "Bambi". "Bambi" at deer camp? Yep. What do you think the world is coming to when a bunch of deer hunters start watching "Bambi" before going hunting?

As I was pondering the effects of this tear-jerker on us tough guys, my thoughts turned to what happened during the first gun season for deer this year. Our oldest daughter, Ruth, after three years, finally hit what she was shooting at.

These past three years as she's gone and hunted with me, I've secretly wondered what her reaction was going to be when and if she killed a deer. Since there's always a mixture of emotions in us when we kill our first one, the possibilities ranged from broken heartedness to elation and everything in between.

Opening Saturday, Ernest Cobb, Hoggie Hargraves, his son-in-law, Mike, and I put up several new stands. One of these was put up with Ruth in mind. Strategically placed on the edge of a secluded soybean field which I had been keeping tabs on for two months, it was the perfect set-up for a new hunter.

Thanks to the FEMAP program through the Department of Wildlife, we had enough doe tags to permit our young folks to kill a doe if no buck was around. Knowing that does entered this field about thirty minutes before black dark every afternoon, I informed

214

said daughter of the most likely spot for the deer to appear and the approximate time to expect them.

As if on cue, two does materialized before her eyes. She eased the rifle up as she had been directed, took careful aim, and squeezed the trigger. The deer she was shooting at made several rapid turns and fled out of the field through a thick switchcane thicket.

When I heard the shot, middle daughter, Joy, and I hurried to check on Ruth. She was out of her stand, shaking, and unsure as to whether or not she had hit anything. A quick check produced sign that the deer had indeed been hit, so we drove back to the camp to get help.

Nearly everyone in camp turned out to assist in tracking Ruth's first. Barely fifty yards from the point of impact, a warhoop went up. The merry-making sounded like a particular TV show in which the characters are always saying something that sounds like, "ROOOOTH, there she is!"

The wait for her reaction wasn't long. She was thrilled. A perfect shot had put deer meat on the table for the Wiman family, and for the first time since I started deer hunting, it wasn't me that furnished the meat. Way to go, Ruth!

As we drove home that evening with the meat, she leaned forward and asked, "When are we going again?"

"As soon as we can."

"Good. I want to kill a buck now! You can put me in a stand and tell me when a buck will show up and where to look for him, can't you?" (Don't you just love it when people have such confidence in you?)

Naturally, Ruth received congratulations and accusations. Some of our good friends asked her if she was ashamed for killing Bambi's mom. She said, "I sure am sorry I killed Bambi's mom...NOT! In fact, I'm going back to get his daddy as soon as I can."

Ah yes, another true hunter is born, and what a thrill it has been for both daughter and father. I don't know which one of us has been the proudest of her. All I hope is that whether it's hunting, fishing, or some other outdoor activity you love, you'll get out and spend some time with your children and grandchildren.

If we can instill respect for and appreciation of the great outdoors along with the thrill of the hunt and the satisfaction of a well-placed shot, we will do a great deal toward solving the problems of crime and drug abuse.

Taking a young person hunting may be a long shot for you, but...

Whatever you do, don't be afraid to go with the long shots. Live life to its fullest every moment and be ready!

"And the Lord God formed man of the dust of the ground, and breathed into his nostrils the breath of life; and man became a living being." (Genesis 2:7)

SNORING

What does a National Guard barracks have in common with a deer camp? Put a group of men together in either of these two settings, add a little fatigue (no pun on the Guard intended), a dash of sinus blockage, and guess what you get? Trophy snoring competition, that's what!

In my short but storied lifetime, I've known some champion snorers. Naturally, I couldn't possibly mention any names in this column. It might embarrass someone, don't you see?

Just for the fun of it, though, let me share some amusing incidents from the National Guard and the deer camps I've known over the years.

It was summer maneuvers for the National Guard at Camp Shelby. One particular sergeant arrived late at night not knowing where the unit from Belzoni was billeted. As our sergeant opened the car door, the mystery was immediately solved. Thanks to the concrete block walls of the barracks, the magnification was so incredible it filled the humid night air with the sound of at least 25 chain saws! From what I've been told, Gum Popper was cutting more logs than all the others combined.

Like I said, we won't mention any names here, so I'll move on to a deer camp I visited near Bruce. The bedroom was filled with bunk beds and could accommodate at least 50 hunters. Having been warned by the gentleman I was hunting with that I should retire as early as possible due to the fact that some of the men snored a bit, I took his advice.

As usual, though tired and in bed a half hour before anyone else, I couldn't get to sleep. I tossed and turned, rolled and fidgeted. Just as I was about to fall asleep, from somewhere in the darkness came a terrible noise. It wasn't the usual rhythmic cadence of most snoring. I was nearly in tears. The man sounded like he was dying!

Sometime around midnight, I finally got up and went into

the other room. The huge wood burning heater had gone out, and icicles were already forming around my tear-stained eyes. After several failed attempts at lighting the fire (not a Boy Scout in those days), gasoline did the trick. Of course, the WHOOMP that broke the stillness of the night sort of interrupted the snoring in the other room. Hiding in the bathroom as everyone rushed in to see what had happened, I slipped through the crowd and was back in my bunk before anyone identified me as the explosives expert. It only took one turn, and I was fast asleep!

Snoring comes in many varieties. There are the polite snorers. Theirs is soft, consistent, and rather pleasant after a while. These polite folks don't snore all the time, only when they're really tired or ill. That's me! I only snore when I'm really tired or have a cold.

Then there are those who snore with a vengeance. I've known several of these types. One of our Assistant Scoutmasters is of this flavor. So, we ask Tag Reed to sleep with him on camping trips. After the first time in a tent with this unnamed individual, Tag said, "Ya'll didn't do me any favors putting me in the tent with Big Daddy (no names, remember?). He made the ground shake!" Now folks, that's snoring!

Just the other night, with only four of us at the deer camp, Greg Eby had to get up in the middle of the night and go to the den. It seems that some sleep "hog" was snoring so loud and so inconsistently that it was impossible for Greg to get to sleep. The snoring bothered him, but when the hog stopped, he wondered if the man had died. It was really frustrating for the newcomer to the camp. The next morning, Greg told Ernest and me that he didn't know a human being could make such noises.

Snoring is a fact of life for many of us. Whether it's loud, long, raucous, and frighteningly without rhythm or soft, consistent, and polite, snoring can be a real thorn in the flesh for the person who doesn't know the joy of waking up refreshed but with a sore throat!

If getting to sleep around someone who snores is a long shot for you, then...

Whatever you do, don't be afraid to go with the long shots. Live life to its fullest every moment and be ready!

"Have I not commanded you? Be strong and of good courage; do not be afraid, nor be dismayed, for the Lord your God is with you wherever you go." (Joshua 1:9)

RAINY DAY BLUES

It's one of those rainy, dreary days of winter. Depressing, aren't they? The sky is grey and dropping rain like a woman's tears during a sad movie. Men don't get emotional like that. Do we, men?

Well, I have to confess that Dorothy almost caught me crying at a movie once. "Where the Red Fern Grows" was almost too much for me. I did manage to cry out of only one eye, the one that was furthest from her view.

Anyhow, days when the pressure and temperature are falling, and the clouds part with a slow, steady drizzle, I get down. It's too nasty to hunt, even ducks! Now folks, I'm talking about a major case of depression here.

What do you do when it sets in to raining before daylight and never quits all day long? Some folks brave the elements and go shopping. Shopping is depressing enough for me, much less on a dreary, down-in-the-mouth day!

Other folks take care of inside stuff. That way, when the weather improves, they can get out again and do all the things they wish they could be doing while it's raining. Now that's the approach I like to take.

What kind of activities can a faithful outdoorsman engage in on a cold, rainy day? Well, might I be so bold as to suggest that you could read a good outdoor humor book by an award-winning author. If you've already read one of those (Tired Tubes and Ten-Speed Turkeys), then you could save this one for a rainy day, or even try some other book, but probably not with as much enjoyment as you're experiencing at this present moment. Right? Yeah, I knew you'd agree.

I don't know about you, but I always have some correspondence I need to catch up on. Alexander Graham Bell almost put me out of the letter writing business, but I've gotten back into it of late. There's always an old hunting buddy who's moved to some

219

great place out west that you really ought to check on.

Such thoughtfulness might even result in an invitation for an elk, muledeer, or antelope hunt next fall. You never know until you try. It beats sitting around being depressed all day, doesn't it? Naturally, the old hunting equipment and clothing could use some mid-season attention. Rifles and shotguns could always use another good cleaning. Well, maybe a good rub down with gun oil will do. The rain might not last that long anyway.

The muddy boots you threw in the utility room tend to get neglected a bit and could use some scraping and beating to dislodge the ever-sticky gumbo or whatever kind of sticky mud you have in your neck of the woods. "How did my boots get in that kind of shape?" you ask. Well, I don't know about you, but I have enough different types of hunting boots so that I just change when the mud gets too bad. That way I have something to do on rainy days, don't you see?

From about mid-December to mid-January, the clothes get mixed up and need sorting out. The blaze orange deer hunting clothes have integrated with the camo duck hunting clothes. This is a very serious situation, people! Ducks are wary creatures anyway, much less when one is wearing a bright orange hat and vest.

Without the blaze orange on a deer hunt, two dilemmas are facing the hunter. It's illegal and worse, it's dangerous. Sorting things out in the hunting closet is sure important and a great job for a rainy day.

A quick check of my calendar on a dreary day usually reminds me that I have certain important events and deadlines coming up. The New Year's Eve duck hunt means I need to check and see if I have plenty of that despicable steel shot and my duck stamps. The annual January duck hunt in Tunica County beckons me to make sure my waders aren't leaking and my extra shotgun is properly plugged.

As for deadlines, well there are the plans for church activities coming up, speaking engagements I committed to in between the end of quail season and the beginning of turkey season. Most assuredly, I mustn't forget the deadline for the newspaper articles I've promised to various papers around the Delta.

Writing has always been a love of mine, and rainy days are perfect for writing. The natural change in emotions on such days seems to start the creative juices flowing, and I love it when a new idea comes together. As you can tell, we haven't had very many rainy days lately!

Being the thoughtful, considerate person that I am, and even though I run the risk of upsetting some of my hunting buddies, a good activity for rainy days would be helping the wife with some of the cleaning chores. There are always clothes to wash, shirts to iron, carpets to vacuum, furniture to polish, bathrooms to clean, and carports to sweep. If you prefer some of the above-mentioned activities over such female jobs, then take your male chauvinistic self to the telephone and hire yourself a housekeeper and be that way!

Surely, finding something worthwhile to do on depressing, dreary, rainy days won't be a long shot for you, but even if it is...

Whatever you do, don't be afraid to go with the long shots. Live life to its fullest every moment and be ready!

"And the swine, though it divides the hoof, having cloven hooves, yet does not chew the cud, is unclean to you." (Leviticus 11:7)

CHITTLINS

I wonder how many of you dear folks have ever been to a chitterling supper. If you have, did you like the main course? To my knowledge (which is limited and diminishing with each passing year!), a chitterling has never passed my lips, tickled my teeth, or slid down my throat.

For those of you whose culinary experience, like mine, hasn't included this delicacy, let me explain what a chitterling is. It's that part of the hog that no sane human being would intentionally eat!

Webster's trusty dictionary gives the following helpful definitions. "Chitter" is a verb which means "to shiver with cold." That sure explains why I get the cold chills everytime someone even mentions cooking the nasty things at deer camp.

"Chitterlings" are defined as: "the small intestine of pigs, used for food." My question is "Why?" Why on earth use something as disgusting as intestines for food? With all that ham, bacon, pork loins, pork chops, pork roast, and all, why do people eat the innards? Yuk!

I reckon folks will eat just about anything, even if they aren't that hungry. Pigs feet, snouts, and brains are on some folks' list of favorite foods, so I guess chitterlings might as well be there, too.

Whenever this particular item is discussed at camp, several matters get talked about in rapid succession. First, "If Ernest and Hoggie are gonna cook chittlins, I ain't coming!" is Leon Cobb's comment. This declaration is quickly seconded by everyone else in on the conversation.

After we've all stated our intentions to be as far removed as possible from the premises when the stinking concoction starts brewing, our thoughts turn to a cooking that occured several years ago at the camp.

One Saturday afternoon when rain was coming down in buckets, it was decided that chittlins would be good for supper. The culprits procured 40-50 pounds of the slimy, disgusting things and washed them thoroughly (something you better do real well if you're gonna fool with chittlins). Then they put them in a pressure cooker, turned on the propane burner, and went back in the camp house.

An exciting game of cards got going, and the card playing chittlin cookers forgot about their boiling brew on the porch. The forgetters got a rude awakening when the top blew off the pressure cooker!

Running out on the front porch, they met an awesome sight. Chittlins were hanging on the limbs of a nearby cedar tree. Chittlins were draped over the rafters above the porch, stretched out on the hood of the nearest pickup and several sections were scattered about on the porch and out in the yard. Those who had begun to imbibe a tad too much volunteered to straighten out the mess and proceeded to pick up the chittlins, wash them off with a water hose, and put them back in the cooker, getting the temperature setting right this time.

No one can remember how they tasted, although a few of those who ate supper that night have a mild recollection that those who ate the most chittlins tasted the most grit! If there's anything worse than boiled chittlins (which I can't imagine), it would have to be gritty boiled chittlins. Yuk, yuk, and double yuk!

For those of you who are devotees of the small intestine of a pig, all I have to say is, "You won't run short on my account." In my case, eating animal insides is a real long shot, and if it is for you, too...

Whatever you do, whether you eat chitterlings or not, don't be afraid to go with the long shots. Live life to its fullest every moment and be ready!

"For him who is joined to all the living there is hope, for a living dog is better than a dead lion." (Ecclesiastes 9:4)

TRIBUTE TO DUKE

Dog lovers realize how special a canine family member can be. Dogs can honestly be man's best friend. Dogs listen without comment or criticism, at least most of the time they do. No matter what deep, dark secret is shared, mum's the word. Even when they're sharply spoken to or spanked, they love their master. Dogs are something very, very special.

When it comes to hunting dogs, most hunters are really blessed if they have one in a lifetime that stands out as "the best ever." In my short lifetime, I've already had several that fit the bill.

Several years back, I had the privilege of keeping a dog for a young man. Due to circumstances beyond his control, he didn't have a place for his black lab named Duke. I offered to take care of the fine animal, provided I could hunt him when the time came. The deal was struck, and Duke came to live at the Wiman residence.

Duke was one duck hunting fool. He loved it as much as I do. Whenever he saw the light come on at four in the morning, his motor was already running when I reached the kennel. The sight of waders and a shotgun was almost more than he could bear. If there was any thought at all of leaving him behind, well, he had ways of showing his displeasure.

On one particular miserably cold morning, Eddie Toney, Duke, and I enjoyed a successful hunt. When we arrived at our spot, the water was frozen, but a few kicks and the decoys had a place to frolic.

After a couple of hours, the lake had frozen over again, so when a couple of mallards fell to our expert aim, Duke immediately started for the pair of greenheads. The ice broke fairly easily as Duke made his way through the decoys, but beyond the decoys, the ice was much thicker.

One of the ducks was trying to get away. Each time Duke would lunge for the duck, it slid away from him on the ice. Obviously aggravated, Duke began to beat the ice ahead of him with his front feet. He literally pounded the frozen water like an

Artic icebreaker until he caught the duck. Then he made his way to the second duck. The sight of Duke with a mallard hanging out of each side of his mouth is one that neither Eddie nor I will ever forget.

On another occasion, Bill Allen and I were duck hunting, when Bill dropped a teal with one heck of a shot. "How good a shot?" you ask. That bird was going so fast that Bill shot him as he crossed the river from Arkansas, and the duck fell in Alabama! Seriously, Bill led the duck by ten to fifteen feet, and it fell over a hundred yards away, still quite alive.

Duke had marked the bird as it fell and was shivering with excitement when I gave him the command to go get the bird. "He'll never get that one," Bill bemoaned.

"Just you wait and see."

Duke reached the duck and, typically, it dove under. Duke looked surprised for a moment and treaded water, watching here and there for the duck to surface.

Momentarily the duck popped up a short distance away. Duke plowed ahead through the water and just as he reached the green-winged teal, it dove under again.

After a couple more similar episodes, Duke had enough of this feathery fiend. When the duck went under for the fifth or sixth time, so did Duke. After a couple of anxious moments, Duke, duck, and soybean stalk all burst through the surface like a submarine-launched missile. The sight of Duke diving under water for that teal is a sight that Bill and I will never forget.

Even though I've owned and hunted with other fine labs, Duke was always doing something incredible, some might even say impossible. My brother came up one duck season for a special hunt on some catfish ponds, which had become a magnet for Canvas-back ducks. These 100-point ducks are large and trophies for those fortunate enough to get one.

That morning, Sonny and I were hunting separate ponds. I had thrown out a few mallard decoys in hopes and had been sitting idle for quite a while when I heard Sonny's shotgun fire twice. In a matter of minutes, he came running down the levee toward me.

"Let's go!"

"Why? What's wrong?"

"I just shot two geese!"

"SOOO?"

"So, it ain't goose season. Let's get out of here!"

First, I mentioned in passing that it was goose season, which helped calm brother's nerves. Second, because he was now worried that the birds were out in the middle of the pond and too far to wade out and retrieve, I told him Duke would go get the geese.

"No way. That dog won't go get something he never saw fall."

"You just watch."

"Duke..." His ears went up and his eyes danced like Fred Astaire. "Mark!" and I pointed toward the spots on the water. The dog's attention was riveted like white on rice. "Back!!!" Duke hit the water and began swimming. He never wavered one degree off the mark. First one, and then the other of the geese (they were ducks by the way) were retrieved. It was an unbelievable sight to watch those two blind retrieves.

Now, I thought Duke had done the ultimate that day. He retrieved those two ducks and picked up my decoys for me (something he really hated to do and always looked at me like I was really being absurd asking him to pick up plastic ducks), but the absolute ultimate feat was carried out for his original owner, Tommy Ashworth.

Hunting on Barnett Reservoir, Tommy knocked down a duck that sailed a long way before falling and then began swimming off. Knowing Duke's amazing abilities, he didn't hesitate to send the dog after the duck. Duke took off and went completely out of sight across the waves. Darkness fell and no Duke. Tommy called and called and finally gave up. With a great deal of sadness, he boated back to the landing and loaded up. As he was driving off, he saw something come up out of the lake and stop on the edge of the road. The headlights illuminated Duke, breathing heavily and obviously worn out — and the duck, still kicking and flopping in Duke's mouth! What a dog!

As Duke grew older, his heart was still in the hunt, but his body began to fail. He developed a common malady among labs called hip displacia. Every time he went into the ice-cold water for a duck, he'd stiffen up. Aspirins helped for a while. Later it took shots. Finally, he was in so much pain that he whined almost on a daily basis.

Putting a dog to sleep is one of the hardest things in the world to do. No matter whether the animal is a house pet or a hunting dog, the emotions are the same. It hurts like — well, like hitting your thumb with a hammer.

Duke's career here on earth has ended. Instead of me, his original owner had to endure the pain of his last days. My heart goes out to you, Tommy. Duke was the finest lab I've ever had the privilege of sharing a duck blind with. He would've killed himself trying to retrieve a duck for me rather than come back with an empty mouth. I can still see him sitting next to me in the blind, the perfect picture of what a Labrador Retriever is supposed to be. Owning a truly fine hunting dog may be a long shot for you, but...

Whatever you do, don't be afraid to go with the long shots. Live life to its fullest every moment and be ready!

"And we know that all things work together for good to those who love God, to those who are called according to His purpose."

(Romans 8:28)

LIVING ON THE RAGGED EDGE

I feel sorry for the dear souls who never try anything new, do the unusual, or take a chance now and then.

Certainly, no one would accuse me of playing it safe. An example of my chance taking way of life? Why certainly!

Imagine a friend who comes down with Lyme Disease, which aggravates the broken back he sustained in a terrible automobile accident. It doesn't help his left knee, which had to be totally reconstructed.

Now, mix in two major house fires, a tornado, and delays of some three months in the publication of four new books; and all of this happened within six months of one another.

Now imagine another friend, son of the above-mentioned recipient of trials and tribulations. In the space of six months, he had undergone shoulder, knee, and foot surgery to repair a separation, torn ligaments, and a multiple fracture. Along the way, he also managed to somehow poison, on accident of course, his dear ole dad.

Now then, here comes the part about taking chances. These two special friends invited yours truly to go duck hunting with them.

I did not ask myself, "Do I want to risk my life going to the woods with the two newest nominees to the Guiness Book of World Records for most catastrophes in a single year for one father/son duet?"

Do I like to live dangerously, or what? Not really, but now and then I do like to take a few chances. It keeps life interesting.

Yes, I went. No, I didn't kill a duck. But, the best part is, nothing terrible happened—if you don't count the fall in the icy water, the flat tire, the stuck truck, or the missed appointment which involved the purchase of the wife's Christmas gift.

No big deal. I dried out. The tire got fixed. The truck got pulled out, and the appointment was kept two days before Christmas.

Things have a way of working out, even when you take chances and go with the long shots, so...

Whatever you do, don't be afraid to go with the long shots. Live life to its fullest every moment and be ready!

"When it is evening you say, 'It will be fair weather, for the sky is red;' and in the morning, 'It will be foul weather today, for the sky is red and threatening.' Hypocrites! You know how to discern the face of the sky, but you cannot discern the signs of the times."

(Mattthew 16:2b-3)

SIGNS

Signs are such interesting and important features of the landscape. Where would we be without signs? When would we know that we're supposed to stop, yield, watch out for deer running across the highway? How would we ever find such remote parts of the globe as the other side of Mobile, Alabama, if it weren't for signs? In my case, even with proper signs, it's down at the docks and on the wrong side of the tunnel under Mobile Bay!

Federal, state, and local authorities go to a whole lot of expense to make sure that we have all the signs we need to get where we want to go and get there safely. The way most of us respond to the messages on road signs, however, makes me marvel at the fact that we ever arrive at our intended destinations.

What I mean by that is the way we ignore the speed limit signs. Now, calm down. I realize that I just quit preaching and went to meddling, but let me continue. If we ignored the sign which pointed north to Memphis the way so many of us ignore the sign that says "Speed Limit: 55-mph," how many of us would ever see the sign to I-40? Odds are, only about half, because the other half of us would wind up in Jackson!

See what I mean? We ignore signs so much of the time. Ever notice what happens when someone puts a sign on a park

230

bench, "Wet paint!"? Nearly everyone who walks by has to stop and feel to see if the paint really is wet.

See what I mean? And how about the signs that read, "Police Line: DO NOT CROSS?" Everyone who can drive, ride a bicycle, or walk a half mile has to go by and get in the way to see what's going on.

And how about those signs that read, "Handicap Parking Only?" Just ask our local Vietnam War Vet, Sammy Bridgers, about the way people ignore that one. I know how you feel, Sammy. When I drive down to the hospital in Jackson and start to pull into a parking place with the sign, "Ministerial Parking Only," and some 330-pound female wearing size 6 leotards pulls in ahead of me and jumps out to go see her boyfriend...

See what I mean? Signs are vitally important to the smooth flow of life in our complicated world, and it upsets the apple cart for us to ignore them the way we do.

Sometimes signs can be humorous, especially homemade ones. During deer season, it isn't unusual to meet people on the back roads of Mississippi looking for their dogs. When a long-legged walker hound gets behind a big old buck, he might end up 20 miles away from where he was turned out.

Some of us rounded a curve this past deer season to find a crude sign swaying gently back and forth in the breeze. Pulling over to take a look at the contents of the message, we learned of a certain individual who had lost his whole pack of dogs.

Dangling from a limb by a seriouly stretched piece of orange survey tape, the sign read, "LOST 1-11-94, 5 Dogs: 1-treeing walker hound/blk with white chest, 2-Tri colored Beagles, 2-Lab Mix-white. If found please call 962-8741 Collect or 834-4519 Local." Having done our share of riding and looking for lost dogs, this note struck us as being a bit humorous. "PLEASE call," the note read. With just a week left in the season, I could understand the urgency! For all I know, the dogs may still be missing, so if you see any dogs matching the above graphic description, heed the sign and give the man a call.

Maybe that sign didn't hit you the way it hit those of us who hunt with dogs, but surely you've seen the truly humorous sign

along the highway, "Men Working?" Just kidding! H e e d i n g
signs like "Do Not Enter" or "Speed Limit 35" might be and most
certainly are long shots for too many of us, but...

Whatever you do, don't be afraid to go with the long shots.
Live life to its fullest every moment and be ready!

"And it came to pass in those days that a decree went out from Caesar Augustus that all the world should be registered. This census first took place while Quirinius was governing Syria. So all went to be registered, everyone to his own city. And Joseph also went up from Galilee, out of the city of Nazareth, into Judea, to the city of David, which is called Bethlehem, because he was of the house and lineage of David, to be registered with Mary, his betrothed wife, who was with child. So it was, that while they were there, the days were completed for her to be delivered. And she brought forth her firstborn Son, and wrapped Him in swaddling clothes, and laid Him in a manger, because there was no room for them in the inn.(Luke 2:1-7)

THE CHRISTMAS LIST

If you haven't made your Christmas list yet, and it's already December 24, then guess what? You're in trouble, my friend. I guess you could always get an early start on next year!

My list this year was a short one. In this land of plenty, I already have everything I need and more of what I want than anyone should.

If you have an outdoorsman in your house, here are some items that might appear on his or her list. No matter how many rifles or shotguns there are in the gun cabinet, there's room for another. A brand new Remington .243 Youth Model Seven rifle found its way into our house for Christmas a couple of years ago, and there's a story to go with it. You sort of figured there would be, didn't you?

A number of years ago, I tried the Patrick McManus metamorphosis trick on Dorothy. The Scouts went on a trip to Missouri during spring break, and one of the stops we made happened to be at the Bass Pro Shop in Springfield. That place is every hunter and fisherman's dream come true. Absolutely out of sight!

While there, I purchased a new shotgun. In order to maintain marital bliss, I explained its presence to Dorothy in terms of a miraculous structural change. The diamond bracelet which I purchased in Branson was mysteriously transformed in the darkness of the vehicle's trunk into a Remington 870 3 inch magnum turkey gun.

Nary a word was uttered in disagreement with my explanation, which should have forewarned me of future consequences. The response I secretly feared and anticipated came when Ruth mentioned to her mother that she really wanted a new watch for Christmas. Dorothy pointed at the new rifle residing in the gun cabinet and said, "Sorry, but it miraculously turned into a rifle."

Before I stir up too many bad memories, I better move on to the Christmas list I'm supposed to be writing about. Other items on a hunter's list might include the newest in footwear for cold weather. Perhaps the latest innovation in game calls for deer, duck, or turkey would be appropriate. No doubt, a set of decoys or a new lab puppy would be nice. The list is endless. Just pick up a catalog from Cabella's, Gander Mountain, The Bass Pro Shop, Tidewater Specialties (just to mention a few) and you'll be in business. You'll be a hit with any hunter on your list with purchases from any one of these.

Having gotten those matters out of the way, let me change gears for a few minutes. No matter what time of year you're kicked back, reading this chapter, one of these days it's going to be Christmas. Maybe the day has come and gone. If it has, you were probably neck deep in wrapping paper and boxes before you discovered these gems of information, but take heart. There's always next year!

Think about it for a minute. Christmas is not only more than presents and parties, trees and treats, family and fun, it's less. Take away all the presents under the tree. For that matter, take away the tree. Take away all the parties and the fattening food. Take away all the hub-bub and hoopla. Now what do we have? We still have Christmas.

Christmas is the day we celebrate the birth of Jesus Christ. Now, I realize that not everybody believes that Jesus is the Messiah, the Son of the Holy Spirit and the Virgin Mary of Isaiah 7, the Ancient of Days of Daniel 7, the Suffering Servant of Isaiah 53, but if a whole lot of us didn't believe that Jesus is our Lord and Savior, we wouldn't have Christmas.

The Light of the World wouldn't have come to illuminate our lives. The Bread of Heaven wouldn't have come to meet our most basic needs. The Good Shepherd wouldn't have come to guide us along the way toward eternity. The Vine wouldn't have come to make our lives sweeter and to empower us to live for the glory of God. The One who is the Way, the Truth, and the Life, would not have come. We would be lost, without hope. Life would be meaningless. We wouldn't be celebrating Christmas at all if Jesus had not come.

For nearly 2,000 years people have believed in, loved, worshipped, followed, and testified to the reality of Jesus. He has changed my life forever. For me, Christmas is nothing without Jesus. With Him, my list is complete. Truth is, with Jesus, I honestly don't need anything else.

Hopefully, this straightforward testimony will not offend any of you. I truly believe that Christmas will be all you want it to be if you add just one more item to your list. Why not ask in the privacy of your own heart for the gift of life through faith in Jesus? If you'll ask Him into your life, He'll come in.

Having a gloriously happy and merry Christmas may be a long shot for some of you, but...

Whatever you do, don't be afraid to go with the long shots. Live life to its fullest every moment and be ready!

"Do you know the time when the wild mountain goats bear young? Or can you mark when the deer gives birth? Can you number the months that they fulfill? Or do you know the time when they bear young? They bow down, they bring forth their young, they deliver their offspring. Their young ones are healthy, they grow strong with grain; they depart and do not return to them." (Job 39:1-4)

IT'S WORTH SAVING

As the new year dawns here in the Mississippi Delta, I believe it's a good time for a bit of reflecting back and thinking ahead. Perhaps reminiscing about the past will help us plan for the future.

In days gone by, this part of the world was nothing but deep woods, a wild untamed reservoir of wildlife and beautiful scenery. Moss-covered cypress and Tupelo gums, like giant gray ghosts of Confederate soldiers, stood guard like silent sentinels over a world virtually unchanged since the dawn of creation.

Then came crosscut saws, and later chain saws and bulldozers. This pristine wilderness took on the appearance of Hiroshima, Japan, following the nuclear blast at the end of World War II. Those who cleared the land had good intentions, for they knew it held the potential of being the most productive agricultural region in the nation, and so it has been for generations now.

In our constant desire to improve on that which was already at its best, we built levees to keep out the spring floods. This meant we could live here instead of only visiting briefly during the dry summer months, but it also meant that the annual revitalization of the land by receding flood waters was no longer possible. Keeping this rich land producing abundantly required commercial fertilizers. Without realizing it, we began to reclaim land that needed to be left alone because the available acreage couldn't keep producing at its former levels.

As we draw near the end of the 20th century, however, we have begun to realize that some of this gumbo ground should have remained as God created it. But this is neither the time to judge our forefathers nor point an accusing finger at anyone. Now's the time

236

to thank God for what He has given us in the natural resources of our Delta bottomlands and try to recover some of its former wealth and beauty.

Thanks to the vision and financial commitments of state and federal agencies, especially the Delta Wildlife Foundation, we have an opportunity before us to bring healing to our land. If marginal land continues to be enrolled in the CRP program and planted in hardwood timber, we may once again enjoy the splendor of Dixieland.

As I speak with landowners and hunters around the Mississippi Delta, I'm encouraged by what I hear and see. We're beginning to understand that productive farming operations need to pay as much attention to the environment as to the bottom line. If we exploit our wildlife, ignore the impact of abusing chemicals, and employ poor farming practices, not only will the environment suffer but so will the economy of our land. Truth is, the Delta is still a rich and wonderful place to live, work, and play. The mountains have their beauty, as do the great plains, sandy beaches, and rugged coastlines of our great nation. To my knowledge, however, there is no elegance quite like that of a brilliant sunset over the Mississippi River. Deer, turkey, and ducks abound in many other regions of America, but I can't think of anywhere I'd rather observe a graceful doe with her fawn, a regal buck checking the wind for danger, a strutting tom turkey, or hear the feeding call of a thousand mallards than from the stillness of a beautiful Mississippi Delta hardwood forest.

Reclaiming the awesome splendor of past eons isn't all that much of a long shot anymore. But even if it was a monumental task, humanly impossible...

Don't be afraid to go with the long shots. Live life to its fullest every moment and be ready!

"Let us hear the conclusion of the whole matter: `Fear God and keep His commandments, for this is the whole duty of man.' For God will bring every work into judgment, including every secret thing, whether it is good or whether it is evil."

(Ecclesiastes 12:13-14)

EPILOGUE

In our rounds together in this adventure, we've passed through the seasons of the year. We've reminisced about the events of the changing months of years gone by, and I hope that you've become a kindred spirit with me in these travels. Family, friends, and the delightful gifts of the great outdoors are ours to enjoy — all gifts from the hand of a generous Benefactor.

As we move along through the changing seasons of time, political correctness demands that we who are Christians should keep that to ourselves. We mustn't publicly proclaim that the God of the Bible is the Creator, Sustainer, and Law Giver, that we are all responsible creatures, made in His image, and accountable to Him.

Since I've never been accused of being politically correct anyway, please pause for a moment as we close to consider this question. If there is a god, and if that god is the God of the Bible, and if you were to stand before Him and He ask you, "Why should I let you into my heaven?" What would you say?

You who revel in God's great outdoors, you who derive such pleasure from the company of like-minded sportsmen as yourself, you who witness God's incredible artistic skill at sunset, you who have experienced the great order of things, can you honestly doubt that God is? And since He is, can there be any doubt that He is the God of the Bible? And since He is the God of the Bible, can there be any doubt that there is but one way to know Him?

Jesus Christ is God in the flesh, the only way to know God personally and thus to have eternal life with God. In John 14:6 Jesus said, "I am the way, the truth, and the life; no one comes to the Father but by me." Though politically incorrect, Jesus is the one and only true God and Savior of mankind.

If you want to become personally acquainted with the one whose marvelous creation you've enjoyed over and over again, then it must be through Jesus Christ. You must come to Him admitting that you aren't good enough to merit His grace but, nevertheless, you desire forgiveness, which is His alone to give. Ask Him to come into your heart and be your Lord and Savior.

Take that step of faith. You will step through a door into life like you've never known it before. Blessings you never knew existed will suddenly tumble into your awareness. The great love and care which God has shown you all along will become very obvious to you. What's more, the next time you go to the woods or lake, you'll see wonders you've not seen before, even though they've been there all along. You just didn't have eyes to see them before Jesus corrected your vision.

Listening to the advice and counsel of the Bible and putting your trust in Jesus Christ alone for salvation may be a long shot for you, but...

Whatever you do, don't be afraid to go with the long shots. Live life to its fullest every moment and be ready!